LANGUAGE AND LITERA

Dorothy S. Strickland, FOUND
Celia Genishi and Donna E. Alverma
ADVISORY BOARD: Richard Allington, Kathryn Au, Bernice Cullir
Carole Edelsky, Shirley Brice Heath, Connie Juel, Su

(Continued)

For volumes in the NCRLL Collection (edited by JoBeth Allen and Donna E. Alvermann) and the Practitioners Bookshelf Series (edited by Celia Genishi and Donna E. Alvermann), please visit www.tcpress.com.

Teaching English Today: Advocating Change in the Secondary Curriculum
BARRIE R.C. BARRELL, ROBERTA F. HAMMETT,
JOHN S. MAYHER, & GORDON M. PRADL, EDS.

Bridging the Literacy Achievement Gap, 4–12
DOROTHY S. STRICKLAND & DONNA E. ALVERMANN, EDS.

Crossing the Digital Divide: Race, Writing, and Technology in the Classroom
BARBARA MONROE

Out of This World: Why Literature Matters to Girls
HOLLY VIRGINIA BLACKFORD

Critical Passages: Teaching the Transition to College Composition
KRISTIN DOMBEK & SCOTT HERNDON

Making Race Visible: Literary Research for Cultural Understanding
STUART GREENE & DAWN ABT-PERKINS, EDS.

The Child as Critic: Developing Literacy Through Literature, K–8, Fourth Edition
GLENNA SLOAN

Room for Talk: Teaching and Learning in a Multilingual Kindergarten
REBEKAH FASSLER

Give Them Poetry! A Guide for Sharing Poetry with Children K–8
GLENNA SLOAN

The Brothers and Sisters Learn to Write
ANNE HAAS DYSON

"Just Playing the Part"
CHRISTOPHER WORTHMAN

The Testing Trap
GEORGE HILLOCKS, JR.

School's Out!
GLYNDA HULL & KATHERINE SCHULTZ, EDS.

Reading Lives
DEBORAH HICKS

Inquiry Into Meaning
EDWARD CHITTENDEN & TERRY SALINGER, WITH ANNE M. BUSSIS

"Why Don't They Learn English?"
LUCY TSE

Conversational Borderlands
BETSY RYMES

Inquiry-Based English Instruction
RICHARD BEACH & JAMIE MYERS

The Best for Our Children
MARÍA DE LA LUZ REYES & JOHN J. HALCÓN, EDS.

Language Crossings
KAREN L. OGULNICK, ED.

What Counts as Literacy?
MARGARET GALLEGO & SANDRA HOLLINGSWORTH, EDS.

Beginning Reading and Writing
DOROTHY S. STRICKLAND & LESLEY M. MORROW, EDS.

Reading for Meaning
BARBARA M. TAYLOR, MICHAEL F. GRAVES,
& PAUL VAN DEN BROEK, EDS.

Young Adult Literature and the New Literary Theories
ANNA O. SOTER

Literacy Matters
ROBERT P. YAGELSKI

Children's Inquiry
JUDITH WELLS LINDFORS

Close to Home
JUAN C. GUERRA

On the Brink
SUSAN HYNDS

Life at the Margins
JULIET MERRIFIELD, ET AL.

Literacy for Life
HANNA ARLENE FINGERET & CASSANDRA DRENNON

The Book Club Connection
SUSAN I. MCMAHON & TAFFY E. RAPHAEL, EDS., WITH
VIRGINIA J. GOATLEY & LAURA S. PARDO

Until We Are Strong Together
CAROLINE E. HELLER

Restructuring Schools for Linguistic Diversity
OFELIA B. MIRAMONTES, ADEL NADEAU, & NANCY L. COMMINS

Writing Superheroes
ANNE HAAS DYSON

Opening Dialogue
MARTIN NYSTRAND, ET AL.

Just Girls
MARGARET J. FINDERS

The First R
MICHAEL F. GRAVES, PAUL VAN DEN BROEK, &
BARBARA M. TAYLOR, EDS.

Teaching Writing as Reflective Practice
GEORGE HILLOCKS, JR.

Talking Their Way into Science
KAREN GALLAS

The Languages of Learning
KAREN GALLAS

Partners in Learning
CAROL LYONS, GAY SU PINNELL, & DIANE DEFORD

Social Worlds of Children Learning to Write in an Urban Primary School
ANNE HAAS DYSON

Inside/Outside
MARILYN COCHRAN-SMITH & SUSAN L. LYTLE

Whole Language Plus
COURTNEY B. CAZDEN

Learning to Read
G. BRIAN THOMPSON & TOM NICHOLSON, EDS.

Engaged Reading
JOHN T. GUTHRIE & DONNA E. ALVERMANN

Words Were All We Had

Becoming Biliterate Against the Odds

EDITED BY

María de la Luz Reyes

Foreword by Luis C. Moll

Teachers College
Columbia University
New York and London

Published by Teachers College Press, 1234 Amsterdam Avenue, New York, NY
10027

Library of Congress Cataloging-in-Publication Data

Words were all we had : becoming biliterate against the odds / edited by Maria
    de la Luz Reyes ; foreword by Luis C. Moll.
        p. cm. — (Language and literacy series)
    Includes bibliographical references and index.
    ISBN 978-0-8077-5180-0 (pbk. : alk. paper)
    ISBN 978-0-8077-5181-7 (hardcover : alk. paper)
      1. Education, Bilingual—United States. 2. Bilingualism—United States.
    3. English language—Study and teaching—United States—Spanish speakers.
    4. Native language and education—United States. I. Reyes, María de la Luz.
    LC3731.W64   2011
    370.117′50973—dc22   2010049622

ISBN 978-0-8077-5180-0 (paper)
ISBN 978-0-8077-5181-7 (hardcover)

Printed on acid-free paper
Manufactured in the United States of America

18   17   16   15   14   13   12   11   8   7   6   5   4   3   2   1

To

Leila Sophia Halcón
Lucia Carmen Halcón
Joaquín Victor Jaime

When you are old enough to read this book, I hope you will understand the importance of the bicultural identity you have inherited from your grandparents and that you will make your potential for biliteracy a reality.

Contents

Foreword

It is with great pleasure that I write the Foreword to this wonderful volume. You are about to read elegantly crafted, heartfelt, and insightful autobiographical narratives. They both moved me and instructed me, as few writings have in our field of study. The authors address several important issues in these pages, among them the variability of identities and cultural activities, the hegemony of English and power differentials in schooling, and class positionality and language shift, loss, or recovery. But it is the bringing of their biliteracy to life—all within different and challenging circumstances, all with rich ethnographic-like details, and all with great frankness, honesty, and clarity—that is at the heart of this book.

The topic of biliteracy has fascinated me for years for both personal and professional reasons. I was born and raised in Puerto Rico, and we spoke only Spanish with all family members and friends. It was simply unthinkable to use English with one another; it never happened. English was ever-present, however, as I shall explain, especially in its literate forms. I do remember not knowing how to speak English, but I have scant memories of learning how to speak it. Similarly, I have no recollection of learning how to read or write it, strange as that may seem. But I do recall that my early biliteracy was supported almost *invisibly*, to borrow a term from Hasan (2002), by my father's willingness to buy me comic books in English. He did not care what I was reading, or in which language, as long as I was reading. His intention was, then, not to teach me English, but to get me reading.

My father simply loved books; they enthralled him, and he was an avid and voracious reader. And so were his brothers and sisters. I remember that my father and I visited them almost every Sunday, and my father routinely would haul two or three shopping bags full of paperback books on many topics to trade with his siblings. As he once told me, the issuance of paperbacks was a momentous occasion in his life; it made a wide variety of books available to a family of modest means like ours. Curiously, my father and his siblings read almost exclusively in English, something that I found unremarkable as a child; it was just the way things were, perhaps because of the greater availability and variety of English paperbacks. They were all fluent readers of Spanish, of course, but they had a clear preference for reading in English, although they always talked about the books in Spanish, never in English. I later would associate such literate "border crossings," where one reads a book in one language but discusses it (or writes about it) in the other, with the use of biliteracy as a tool for thinking.

A clear difference between my circumstances and those represented in this book is that I was never scolded or punished for speaking Spanish, not even at the American prep school in San Juan that my mother, not happy with my progress in English, forced me to attend for a few years, much to my dismay. In contrast, most of the present chapters reveal the contradiction of the encouragement at home of becoming bilingual and the disparaging of Spanish in schools in their push to produce English monolinguals, a cowardly and abusive practice still very much in vogue in many schools. There is hardly a Latino child who has not been marked as undesirable by such practices, remnants of colonialism. But what the chapters make clear, and my anecdotes do not, is the resilience of the authors, even as children, in defending what is rightfully theirs, in earning their biliteracy, one could say. What is also clear in every chapter is the powerful role of emotions in language learning. These two related themes, resilience and emotions—constants in the book and of great theoretical importance in understanding language learning—are easy to miss by those who study only English monolingual development.

Torres-Guzmán (2004) has suggested that the development of bilingualism, and especially the literate forms of the languages, as in the present case, represents a manifestation and expression of self-determination for Latinos within the context of the United States. The chapters that follow present biliteracy not simply as language or literacy skills, but as deeply formative, as a way of life, and, I believe, as a form of personal decolonization. And in all the chapters, the centrality of the person, their agency (within particular and shifting conditions for living, and with the language and cultural resources at hand), becomes an indispensable and unforgettable part of the stories.

—Luis C. Moll, University of Arizona

REFERENCES

Hasan, R. (2002). Semiotic mediation and mental development in pluralistic societies: Some implications for tomorrow's schooling. In G. Wells & G. Claxton

(Eds.), *Learning for life in the 21st century: Sociocultural perspectives on the future of education* (pp. 112–126). London: Blackwell.

Torres-Guzmán, M. (2004). Language, culture and literacy in Puerto Rican communities. In B. Pérez, T. McCarty, L. Watahomigie, & M. Torres-Guzmán (Eds.), *Sociocultural contexts of language and literacy* (pp. 111–135). Mahwah, NJ: Lawrence Erlbaum.

Preface

Over the years I have encountered a recurring phenomenon in my studies of bilingual students—an occurrence I call "spontaneous biliteracy." I use the term *spontaneous* in the same way that Clark (1976) and Durkin (1966) use "spontaneous reading" to refer to a child's ability to read without receiving instruction. In my work with Latinos, spontaneous biliteracy signals an individual's ability to move along the oral and literate continuum (Hornberger, 2003) and the monolingual and biliterate continuum in English and Spanish *without prescribed instruction in both languages.* "Spontaneous," however, does not mean biliteracy can be acquired by osmosis. If that were so, all Latinos living in bilingual environments would be biliterate. Unfortunately, this is not the case.

Since I have conducted research solely in transitional bilingual programs, it is in those contexts that I have observed emergent biliteracy—not in dual language models where one might expect it (Reyes, 2001; Reyes, 2004; Reyes & Costanzo, 2002; Reyes, Laliberty, & Orbanosky, 1993). Spontaneous biliteracy was evident in a subset of Mexicano/Latino students, members of a cohort whose literacy development I tracked for 4 years (Kindergarten–3rd grade). Although students were receiving literacy instruction solely in their dominant language, some were emerging as biliterates as early as 1st grade (Reyes, 2001).

Students enrolled in bilingual programs are exposed to two languages whether or not they receive instruction in both. Their participation in a bilingual program provides "creative space" to experiment and engage in language play in two languages. When teachers do not constrain students' explorations, or set up artificial barriers between the two languages, there is potential for emergent biliteracy (Reyes, 2001).

Spontaneous biliteracy also can be found among adult Latinos. While it is easy to understand that biliteracy could be a result of participation in bilingual programs, how is it possible for individuals with no formal instruction in two languages to become biliterate, especially coming from an era when they were punished for using Spanish in school? This question is at the heart of this book.

Words Were All We Had: Becoming Biliterate Against the Odds examines the personal narratives of a select group of Chicana/os[1] and Puerto Rican education professionals who attained biliteracy at an early age and in the era *before* bilingual education. Their stories celebrate and make visible a linguistic potential that has been largely ignored in schools. As such, the narratives represent a sliver of unwritten history of Latina/os' triumph over a school system intent on suppressing non-English languages. Their tenacity and resilience to succeed under less than optimal learning conditions offer hope for students who feel alienated in schools and who struggle to learn in a climate of rejection. Although the authors' journeys through school occurred many years ago, they still mirror the experiences of today's Latino students who must make the false choice between English and Spanish, but must do so in the face of relentless anti-Mexicano, anti-Latino rhetoric surrounding current immigrants.

The focus on Chicanos and Puerto Ricans educated in the period between the mid-1940s through the 1960s is intentional. First, these were the two major Spanish-speaking groups in schools before bilingual education legislation permitted use of non-English languages for instruction. Other Latino groups (e.g., Cuban Americans, Central Americans, and South Americans) were *not* yet enrolled in schools in any significant numbers. Second, these Chicano and Puerto Rican authors represent a generation of *American-born* Spanish speakers from poor working-class families who entered school with fluency in their native language. In a real sense, "words were all they had," yet schools were intent on eradicating their most important vehicle for learning. Against the odds, these individuals became biliterate and succeeded in schools while thousands of others failed. Today, these authors are well-respected educators with considerable knowledge of schools and of Latino students. For this reason their autobiographical accounts provide unique views of how they, as Latino students of another era, navigated the same system that continues to ignore Latinos' linguistic and cultural resources. Writing in narrative rather than in traditional academic style, allows these authors to write with greater freedom and candor. Like core sampling in geology, personal narratives enable readers to examine the various layers of experiences, strategies, adaptive behaviors, and diverse paths that biliterates forged to balance the "push and pull" of home and school.

This collection is intended to help teachers extrapolate key lessons about the individual potential of *their* young Latino pupils, lessons related to the role of language and culture in students' academic success. As a whole, the narratives represent a range of responses to the ban on Spanish and reveal a variety of factors that supported or impeded the authors' academic efforts. They illustrate little-known, nontraditional ways in which parents with limited education influence and motivate their children to do well in school and strive for a better life. They highlight the important role that caring teachers can play in a single instance of a child's life when they praise and encourage students' efforts to reach their full potential, and when they permit Latino students to experiment with the two languages at their disposal.

A CAVEAT

Extolling the acquisition of biliteracy *without* access to bilingual education should not be construed as an argument against bilingual education, any more than acknowledging spontaneous reading calls for a position against reading instruction. On the contrary, the purpose of the book is to celebrate biliteracy, to display the steely determination required to maintain and advance a native language when there is no academic structure to support it. The argument here is: *If biliteracy is possible when all the odds are against it, how much easier would it be if effective bilingual education were an inherent part of the core curricula in schools and available to all?* More students would be truly bilingual and biliterate. Latino students would not have to choose between Spanish and English. Channels of communication between generations, so essential to family cohesion, would remain open instead of rupturing because young children can no longer speak to their elders. Finally, these narratives are intended to provide readers with a close examination of factors that can influence students' learning. It is a way to underscore the irreparable loss of the linguistic potential readily available to Latino students.

NOTE

1. The term *Chicana/o* is used here to refer to the majority of Mexican Americans born in the United States as well as those who self-identify as Chicana/o. This political term also is used as a way of denoting pride in their language and culture; it became popular during the Civil Rights Movement and appears in social science literature referencing that era.

Acknowledgments

The African proverb, "It takes a village to raise a child," is apropos here. Bringing this book to fruition has come about, not solely by my own efforts, but by the efforts and interest of many friends, colleagues, students, acquaintances, and family members. To adequately thank them, I need to start with the many Mexicano, Chicano, and Latino students who have participated in my literacy studies over the years and have sustained my interest in biliteracy. Those studies left me with more questions than answers, specifically in pursuit of answers to how biliteracy can develop without organized instruction, and in a climate of rejection. In 2008, I surveyed a group of about 40 colleagues who responded with serious interest to my survey question. Their responses planted the seed for *Words Were All We Had: Becoming Biliterate Against the Odds*. I thank them for the mini portraits they painted of themselves as children learning to read in Spanish and English.

The contributors and I are honored and thankful to our esteemed friend and colleague, Luis C. Moll, for writing such a thoughtful Foreword to this book. We value his insightful perspective on this work.

Heartfelt thanks go to the busy contributors—all friends and colleagues—who took the time to peel back the layers of personal memories, to uncover how people, events, and conditions contributed to, or detracted from, their biliteracy development: Steven Arvizu, María Balderrama, Lilia Bartolomé, María Fránquiz, Josué González, John Halcón, Carmen Mercado, Sonia Nieto, Pedro Pedraza, and Concepción Valadez. *De todo corazón, gracias*. Additional thanks to Josué, Lilia, and María Balderrama who pointed out or sent me important sources and critical ideas to ponder.

I am indebted to my local reviewers and friends, Greg Armstrong, Rosa Moreno, and Elizabeth Garza, who provided helpful suggestions, raised questions, and demonstrated strong enthusiasm and excitement about the book from beginning to end. A very special thanks to my dear friend and former colleague, Pamela McCollum, for her honest critique of the manuscript as it was evolving, offering helpful suggestions, and making keen observations. Her interest and support for this project buoyed my confidence. Summa cum laude thanks to my husband, John Halcón, a true critic and ever a fan, who listened to my ideas over lunch and dinner, offering critique and support, cheering me on to completion of this project. *Mil gracias a* Josefa (Pepa) Vivancos Hernández for helping me with last-minute technical glitches. Thanks also to Meg Lemke, Acquisitions Editor at TC Press, for her guidance and insightful suggestions, and to the many in-house editors who "blew away the chaff and kept the good grain."

Introduction

María de la Luz Reyes

Growing up bilingual in America should be cause for celebration. Heritage languages are vital national resources, particularly in pluralistic societies. They should be fostered for their intrinsic value, for affirmation of their speakers, and for their benefit to national security. In an era of globalization, when linguistic diversity in the United States is growing exponentially, the need to learn a second language is even more imperative.

The reality, however, is that federal and state policymakers, and school administrators have not perceived bilingualism as particularly efficacious. They have not understood the important link between academic learning and an individual's language, culture, and identity. Historically, schools have treated non-English languages and cultures as obstacles to the assimilationist ideology of schools (Crawford, 1992; U.S. Commission on Civil Rights, 1976). As Nieto (1998) notes, "Although the 'melting pot' has been heralded as the chief metaphor for pluralism in the United States, a rigid Anglo-conformity has been in place for much of U.S. history" (p. 143). An extreme example of this ideology is the near annihilation of native peoples and their ways of life, and extinction of indigenous languages. Those measures have led to devastating consequences for their progeny (Deloria, 1984).

Although Spanish speakers did not endure forcible removal from their homes or transfer to boarding schools, as was the case for Native Americans, they have tolerated years of overt and covert suppression of their native language in schools. Spanish speakers have endured linguistic oppression and limited opportunities for self-expression in their native language. Prohibition of Spanish, along with the corresponding physical and psychological punishment for violating the ban, has contributed to Latino students' cultural ambivalence, creating conflict between the values of home and school (Crawford, 1992; Cummins, 1989). For many, the consequences have been school failure and persistently high drop-out rates (Trueba, 1987).

1

Among current Chicana/o and Puerto Rican education professionals, there is a large number who attended elementary and high school in the era when Spanish was banned in schools. They endured punishment meted out for violating the ban (U.S. Commission on Civil Rights, 1972, 1976). As children, these individuals had no formal instruction to support their acquisition of biliteracy in English *and* Spanish, yet a significant number of them are now bilingual and biliterate.

DEFINITION OF BILITERACY

Biliteracy, as used here, denotes not only an individual's ability to read and write in two languages, but also "any and all instances in which communication occurs in two (or more) languages in or around writing" (Hornberger, 1990, p. 213; see also Hornberger, 2003). There is no attempt here to qualify or quantify the biliteracy of the contributors since these are self-reported assessments of their development of biliteracy, a kind of "indirect measure" of literacy (Macías, 1994, p. 21).

Hornberger's (1990, 2003) conceptual framework, the continua of biliteracy, is useful in understanding the intricacy of biliteracy. Rather than juxtaposing competencies as polar opposites, the framework views those competencies as points along a continuum. Hornberger and Skilton-Sylvester (2003) point out that there is "balanced attention to both ends of the continua and all points in between" (p. 36). The framework utilizes intersecting and nested continua to highlight the complex interrelationships between literacy and bilingualism through which biliteracy emerges. The continua have four nested relationships: contexts, media, content, and development. Within the biliterate contexts are the oral to literate, monolingual to bilingual, and micro to macro continua. Biliterate development includes reception to production, oral to written, and L1 to L2 continua. Biliterate content considers minority to majority, vernacular to literary, and contextualized and decontextualized continua. Finally, biliterate media include divergent to convergent, successive to simultaneous, and similar to dissimilar continua. All dimensions of biliteracy are interrelated and inextricably bound. The continua of biliteracy make clear that there are many points on a continuum that an individual may occupy at any given moment, making the individual a more fluent or less fluent bilingual. Movement on the continuum depends on the social context, the speakers, and other aspects of the social event. The movement is fluid and the "points are not finite, static, or discrete" (Hornberger, 2003, p. 5).

Understanding that biliteracy is on a continuum explains how someone can seem to be a fluent Spanish speaker at one point, and a less fluent speaker at another point, or how an individual can have receptive but not productive skills at another point. The difference is simply that the individual is occupying different points on a specific continuum.

Biliteracy is a dynamic process. The degree of proficiency in more than one language is domain specific, but even in the emerging stages of development, access to two languages often helps one make sense of the other because there is a two-way transfer of knowledge. As Maguire (1999) notes, "Becoming biliterate is a complex, dynamic, relational process. It is situated and distributed, constructed and negotiated" (p. 117).

MAKING IT LOOK EASY

Bilinguals often make bilingualism and biliteracy look easy. Manipulating two distinct linguistic systems, however, is a complex process when one considers differences in phonology, morphology, semantics, syntax, and pragmatics in English and Spanish. The ease with which bilinguals shift codes may be the reason why Latinos rarely are given credit for their linguistic competency, while native English speakers who learn a second language are extolled for their accomplishment (see Nieto, this volume). I also have described this biliteracy phenomenon as "invisible biliteracy," because it almost always goes unnoticed, unappreciated, and unrecognized as a sign of intelligence (Reyes, 2001).

Although experts have argued that learning a language requires that the target language not be stigmatized or "marked" (Fishman, 1976; Griego Jones, 1993), this does not necessarily seem the case in the spontaneous biliteracy of the Latina/os featured in this volume. In fact, Spanish not only was viewed as undesirable, it was officially banned at the time Chicanos and Puerto Ricans were becoming biliterate.

Today, while some Latino students have access to bilingual education classes, there are still not enough programs for all English language learners enrolled in schools. In 2003–2004, only 11% of all English language learners had access to bilingual education services (U.S. Department of Education, 2006). Worse yet, bilingual programs are continually in jeopardy, even more so now that schools are under intense pressure to show academic gains on tests mandated by No Child Left Behind (NCLB). In 2009, the *Yakima Herald-Republic* reported that the Wapato School District had scrapped all dual language classes because the Director of Bilingual Education believed that they no longer "have the time or resources to teach kids Spanish when [they] have to meet (academic) benchmarks" (Ferolito, 2009). With no time in a school day for much more than "teaching to the test," bilingual education, social studies, music, art, and physical education have been downgraded to "diversions" from the task of learning English and scoring high on NCLB tests (Meier & Wood, 2004).

CURRENT LEARNING CONDITIONS FOR LATINO STUDENTS

Despite the existence of bilingual programs, Latino students today, like previous generations of Spanish speakers, still attend a public school system that has not fundamentally changed its goals or its hegemonic structures (Solórzano & Yosso, 2002; Yosso, 2006). Asymmetric power relations between dominant and minority groups have remained static (Bartolomé, 2008b), making it virtually impossible to make significant changes in the system. While schools may no longer have *official* policies banning Spanish, or a system of penalties for students who speak their native language within school premises, non-English languages are still viewed as less prestigious and less important than English. Latino children continue to be labeled "at risk" because they come from homes where a language other than English is spoken.

Furthermore, bilingual programs rarely enjoy the full support of administrators and teachers. The subtext for students is clear: *Your native language and culture are not only irrelevant but a detriment to academic success.* When you add the widespread animus proliferated by the media toward immigrants and Latinos, it becomes clear that learning conditions for Latinos have not changed much over the decades. As Halcón (2001) points out, it is not native language but the negative rhetoric filtering down from the mass media to schools and Latino homes that negatively affects students' self-perceptions and hinders learning.

The Prohibition of Spanish

Prior to passage of bilingual education legislation in 1968, English was the only language permitted in K–12 schools except for foreign language classes. Bilingualism was thought to cause "mental confusion" (Carter, 1970; Gorman, 1973). Puerto Ricans and Chicanos were subjected to ethnic, racial, social, and linguistic discrimination (Del Valle, 1998). Schools forced all non-native English speakers to adopt English and Anglo-American values as a means of "rescuing" them from the disadvantages of their native culture and language, which were believed to hamper learning (San Miguel, 1987, 1999). Prohibiting Spanish was believed to be a means to rapid acculturation. To accomplish that end, school districts in the Southwest, particularly in Texas and California, imposed a comprehensive "No Spanish" rule (Carter, 1970; U.S. Commission on Civil Rights, 1972).

Use of Spanish was barred throughout the school premises. Students found in violation risked one or more of the following disciplinary actions: detention, suspension, school expulsion, grade demerits, monetary fines, and even corporal punishment (Crawford, 1992). The Texas Penal Code went so far as to declare the use of Spanish in school activities a *crime*. As late as 1970 a high school teacher in Crystal City, Texas, was indicted for teaching a history class in Spanish, but the case subsequently was dismissed (U.S. Commission on Civil Rights, 1972). With all the restrictive policies and practices in place, students from Spanish-speaking homes had few or no opportunities to publicly demonstrate cultural pride or advance their Spanish language skills without fear of retribution.

The Case of Puerto Rican Students

As a result of the Spanish-American war of 1898, the island of Puerto Rico was colonized and later appropriated as a territory of the United States. The United States moved quickly to impose English as the primary language of instruction in island schools as a way of assimilating (and controlling) the Spanish-speaking inhabitants. This action met with strong resistance. In 1948, the Puerto Rican government re-instituted Spanish as the language of instruction, but made English a required subject from elementary grades to college (Pausada, 2008). In 1917 the U.S. government granted U.S. citizenship to persons born on the island of Puerto Rico (Dobles & Segarra, 1998). Puerto Ricans, like Chicanos in the Southwest, experienced race, ethnicity, and language discrimination in both mainland and island schools, and an insidious disparagement of their Spanish language variety. Over time, rejection on their native island and on the mainland has led to conflicted loyalties that, in part, contribute to Puerto Rican students' academic problems in school (Nieto, 1998). Migration of students to and from the island has produced a feeling of cultural ambivalence among these students, who feel alienated in both places.

Students' Responses to the Ban on Spanish

Chicano and Puerto Rican students' responses to censure of their language fell into three general categories: acquiescence, resistance, and accommodation (and variations thereof). Students in the acquiescence category complied with the mandate, convinced it was the only path to academic success. Some followed in the footsteps of Richard Rodriguez (*Hunger of Memory*, 1982); they embraced it. Bilingual Latinos consider Rodriguez the "poster boy" for those who foolishly but readily give up their language in exchange for school success. A second category of students responded with strong resistance and anger over the rule. Their defiance provoked on-going reprimands, punishment, personal rejection, and dis-illusionment. Many felt "pushed out" and eventually dropped out. The third category of responses included various forms of accommodation. These students adapted and learned creative ways to "play the game," to adjust to school policies without severing their cultural ties to their families, and without relinquishing their native language or their cultural identity. Responses were as varied and unique as the individuals them-selves. Even siblings attending school with the same teachers had different responses—some acquiesced, some resisted. At times, students fought against the language restrictions; at other times, they acquiesced, depend-ing on the circumstances and agency. Many suspended their public use of Spanish while they were in school, but later worked hard to recover it.

Although the English-only mandate made it increasingly difficult for Latinos to develop academic language in Spanish, and made the devel-opment of biliteracy more unlikely, successful students learned to walk a tightrope between the demands of the school and their own cultural needs. They remained in school and succeeded academically. Two fac-tors may have worked in their favor. One, these students formed a strong cultural identity because they experienced positive interactions with family, institutions, and peers in the native language. Experiencing the vitality of Spanish among people they cared about mitigated the nega-tive perceptions of Spanish so prevalent in schools. Two, guidance from Spanish-literate adults and peers helped them see the use of biliteracy in meaningful, socially important ways (Tse, 2001).

Lack of Organized Efforts to Maintain Spanish

Spanish-speaking groups have no record of organized classes for teaching Spanish, as do other linguistic groups (e.g., Chinese, Koreans, Greeks, Germans, Russians, Polish, Arabs, Jews, Armenians, and other im-migrants), who have established after-school or weekend ethnic language and heritage classes for their children (Bradunas & Toppings, 1988). On the contrary, the only type of organized Spanish instruction outside the traditional school system was the "Little Schools of the 400" established in 1957 by a World War II veteran and President of the League of United Lat-in American Citizens (LULAC). The primary purpose of the Little Schools was to teach the 400 most common *English* words to preschool Mexican American children to prepare them for school (San Miguel, 1987).

Spanish-speaking groups generally have left Spanish language and literacy learning up to individuals, to their families, or to chance. As a con-sequence, by the 2nd or 3rd generation, these groups suffer language loss

(Wong-Fillmore, 1991). Although widespread xenophobia can account for the lack of public concern over the diminution of Spanish, it is undeniably an irreparable loss of language resources for a monolithic nation such as the United States. Other arguments suggest that close proximity to Mexico and Puerto Rico makes Spanish language schools pointless for Spanish-speaking children because constant influx from those regions revitalizes Spanish with each incoming group. This may be true, but without formal instruction, the majority of Spanish speakers may become functional bilinguals, but not necessarily proficient in academic Spanish, or biliterate. On the other hand, having no organized classes does not imply that individuals or families have not encouraged, or do not encourage, maintenance of Spanish, or provide informal instruction and guidance in learning to read and write Spanish, as the various authors here testify.

WHY NARRATIVES?

Although narratives are an important source of knowledge, academics generally dismiss their content as neither empirical nor scientific enough to have value (Trimmer, 1997). Yet, Trimmer contends that personal narratives are our personal truth; they "create the very space that we as a group, any group, inhabit. Place is made by story" (p. 9), and stories are a road to self-discovery. From a historical perspective, first-person accounts of events as viewed through the eyes of those who experienced them are the best way to understand an era. Featherstone (1989) argues that "the telling of stories can be a profound form of scholarship moving serious study close to the frontiers of art in the capacity to express complex truth and moral context in intelligible ways" (p. 377). Narratives, like *testimonios*, also "function as early sites of ideological struggle," where the narrators "reconstruct their past and retrospectively narrate [it]." Additionally, narratives create "a liminal ethnic space produced as much by their particular history" as by the institutionally racist structure of U.S. schools (Sánchez, 1995, p. 1).

The final chapter of this book discusses and analyzes emerging themes from the narratives, using a critical race perspective (Delgado & Stefancic, 2001) or, more specifically, a Latino critical race (LatCrit) lens (Delgado Bernal, 2002; Solórzano & Yosso, 2002; Yosso, 2006). Critical race theory (CRT) has its roots in the belief that race is at the center of American life. It is used here as a framework to challenge "the ways that race and racism implicitly and explicitly shape social structures, practices, and discourses" (Yosso, 2006, p. 4). CRT asserts that the perspectives, values, and assumptions of the dominant majority, which form the "master narrative" by which all members of society are valued and measured, are not the *only* reality. There are other realities that derive from the experiences of members of social and racial minorities (Delgado & Stefancic, 2001). CRT uses storytelling as a method of giving voice to the realities of those nondominant groups. Thus, critical race theory is a particularly efficacious means of examining the narratives in this book. Further, Latina/o critical race theory focuses particularly on Chicana/o and Latina/o consciousness to CRT. It examines "racialized layers of subordination based on immigration status, sexuality, culture, language, phenotype, accent, and surname" (Yosso, 2006, p. 6).

These counterstories (Solórzano & Yosso, 2002) offer a close-up examination of Latinos' experiences in navigating and triumphing over a school system that crushed the spirit of millions of others who dropped out of school over the past 60 years or more.

The following chapters form the collection of narratives. Because all the authors are members of Latino communities who share the same native language, have similar cultural backgrounds, and occupied a subordinate status in the hierarchy of power, there are recurring themes in the chapters. Each story, however, reveals a distinct and unique response to the individual's circumstances. Taken as a whole, their narratives present an illuminating montage of the school experiences of Chicanos and Puerto Ricans in a pre-bilingual education era. Their struggle to attain biliteracy, and remain *whole*, informs our perspectives as educators, not only on the resilience of Latino and other linguistically different students, but on the emotional struggle children experience in remaining faithful to their heritage language and culture. At the same time, the authors' triumph *against the odds* highlights the appalling loss of human potential and cultural resources in hundreds of other students who could not defend themselves against the erasure of their native language.

ABOUT THE BOOK

The book is organized into four parts, described below, with a preview of each chapter.

In Part I, Embracing Biliteracy with Conviction and Purpose, the authors provide recollections of growing up in homes where speaking Spanish was the norm. Although each arrived at biliteracy by a different route and under different sociocultural circumstances, they all share a strong conviction of the importance of biliteracy. They celebrate its richness and detail the efforts they exerted to develop and enhance their dual language competency.

In Chapter 1, Sonia Nieto describes the "sheer panic" of feeling mute in an English-only classroom. An intense need to belong and strong pressure to adopt English and discard Spanish led to her rejection of both her language and Puerto Rican culture. In the end, a recalibration redirected her to a fuller understanding of the principles of biliteracy, and she became an expert in diversity, extolling the promise of biliteracy.

In Chapter 2, Josué González focuses on the wealth of the words he inherited without regard to whether the words were English or Spanish. For him, words could create rich imagery, emotion, joy, love, hope, and passion. He describes growing up in a community where Chicanos formed an integral part of society and where bilingualism was regarded as social capital. His narrative illustrates the natural emergence of biliteracy when two languages are accorded equal respect and worth.

In Chapter 3, Carmen Mercado writes of her "illusory" goal to develop a command of Spanish commensurate with her academic, professional competence in English. She describes how in taking advantage of linguistic opportunities presented to her in New York and Puerto Rico, circumstances and personal relationships with native Spanish speakers served as catalysts to advance her goal. Her journey illustrates her deep conviction of biliteracy, dogged determination, and the personal effort she has exerted to master Spanish when schools have dismissed and suppressed it.

In Part II, *Novelas, Revistas, Fotonovelas*, and Prayer Books: Stepping Stones to Biliteracy, the authors reveal how they learned to read Spanish with available, inexpensive, nontraditional, reading materials. The authors used *novelas, revistas* (informative magazines), or Latin/Spanish prayer books and hymnals in church as textual stepping stones to their emerging literacy in Spanish. Each describes the various steps that led to her biliteracy.

In Chapter 4, Lilia Bartolomé relates how her mother's, her cousin's, and their friends' infectious enthusiasm for reading and trading Mexican *novelas* piqued her own interest in learning to read Spanish. The women in her life regarded reading as essential nourishment, or "comida," and young Lilia wanted to partake. Once her mother taught her the fundamentals of Spanish reading, she plunged into hours of entertainment reading *novelas* and *fotonovelas*, a practice that would lead to her biliteracy.

In Chapter 5, I (María de la Luz Reyes) describe how my family's devout Catholicism frequently placed me in Church where there were plenty of prayer books, missals, and hymnals in Latin, Spanish, and English. In my efforts to fully participate in religious services, I carefully tracked the Spanish words that lay side by side with Latin words until one day I discovered I could read Spanish. When I learned to read English in school, I was a step closer to developing biliteracy.

In Chapter 6, María Balderrama writes about the inseparable link between language and identity. Viewing herself as bilingual and biliterate, she recounts how *cositas de lengua* define and articulate her worldview. Her biliteracy has served her as "armor" against all types of domination. She learned to read Spanish using *revistas*, her aunt's popular women's magazines, and by reading Mexican *novelas* purchased in the border town of Mexicali, Mexico.

In Part III, Resistance, Agency, and Biliteracy, the authors describe the different ways they used cultural agency to remain connected to their Spanish language and culture, but also how they fought against the injustices of English hegemony. The manner in which they contested linguistic injustices was uniquely different. Their role as translators and interpreters also contributed to their bilingual and biliterate competency.

In Chapter 7, John Halcón paints a clear image of the on-going linguistic tug of war between his father, who demanded his children speak English, and his mother, who insisted they learn Spanish to stay connected with their Mexican relatives. John had no choice but to become bilingual and biliterate. His bilingualism earned him good grades and the role of the principal's interpreter, but his loyalty to his mother's language would erupt in a defiant stand against authority that culminated in an elementary school student protest.

In Chapter 8, Steven Arvizu describes his emergence as a young cultural broker in the midst of the hustle and bustle of his mother's cantina/restaurant. Upon his entering school, his mother leaned on him to translate for friends and customers, adults who relied on his bilingual and biliterate skills. Each translating occasion provided him exposure to a broad range of situations, requiring different vocabulary and discourse styles. Steve learned important social, political, and linguistic skills that enabled him to resist the ban on Spanish at the same time that he utilized it to help others.

In Chapter 9, Concepción Valadez, *la nena*, as her parents called her, recounts her early experiences in segregated schools, enduring punishment for speaking Spanish and discrimination against her low socioeconomic status. Despite this, and with the help of her parents, she became biliterate at an early age. When she was rejected, she resisted by persevering and taking charge of her pursuit of academic achievement, as she learned from her parents important lessons in fighting against injustices.

In Part IV, Island and Mainland Influences on Biliteracy, the authors describe how their time in Puerto Rico positively influenced their development of Spanish and fortified their cultural identity. Their experiences in U.S. mainland schools varied. One attended culturally and linguistically diverse public schools in New York City; the other attended Catholic schools in various regions of the South and Southwest where her father was stationed.

In Chapter 10, María Fránquiz recounts growing up in a military family that took her from her native island of Puerto Rico to North Carolina, Germany, Texas, and California. Each move required major personal and cultural adjustments that forced her to acquire a variety of social and linguistic survival skills, as well as fluency and literacy in Spanish and English. María describes her enrollment in various Catholic schools and how those experiences influenced her later life.

In Chapter 11, Pedro Pedraza describes the teeming ethnic and racial diversity of East Harlem where he grew up. Interacting with all these groups required him to use English as his dominant language. His visits to Puerto Rico presented opportunities for developing Spanish fluency and forming deep bonds with his extended family and his Puerto Rican culture. As he matured and returned to the island as a teenager, his bilingual skills eventually solidified and balanced out as he took Spanish classes in high school and college.

The following chapters constitute the heart of the book, showcasing the autobiographical journeys of the authors that reveal rich details (rarely shared by academics or in academic books) about the personal and sociocultural contexts in which their biliteracy developed.

Part I

EMBRACING BILITERACY WITH CONVICTION AND PURPOSE

CHAPTER 1

On Learning to Tie a Bow, and Other Tales of Becoming Biliterate

Sonia Nieto

As a 1st-grader, Sonia Nieto discovered many barriers between her Puerto Rican heritage and her school. Like most immigrants and Spanish-speaking students currently in schools, Sonia learned that her native language had little value, that it was discourteous and unacceptable to speak Spanish in school. The chasm between home and school often creates stress and anxiety for children who want to be accepted and long to be like others. Like Sonia, immigrant children go to great lengths to be like los americanos, *even to the extent of avoiding (or losing) their native language, and feeling ashamed of their family. Fortunately, Sonia returned to her language with conviction and new purpose as she went on to college. Creating an affirming classroom for linguistically diverse students pays better learning dividends. Sonia's chapter reveals how teachers can do this.*

I guess I hadn't learned how to tie a bow before I started school; I don't remember. What I do remember was feeling mute. I had just started school and there I was, a 6-year-old in a 1st-grade classroom in a run-down ghetto school in Brooklyn, trying to tie my hat. I had probably been in the class for a couple of months because the temperature must have been cold (why else would I be wearing a hat?) but evidently I hadn't learned how to let my teacher know I needed help. I stood there, gesturing and making sounds that made no sense to her, attempting to ask her to tie my hat. I felt helpless.

Funny, the memories that stay with you. There is much about my childhood that I do not remember, but this scene is as vivid to me today as if it were yesterday. I suppose my memory says something about the tremendous vulnerability I felt at not being able to make myself understood, the sheer panic of not having language.

I did have language, of course. But the language I had was not the officially sanctioned language of school. At home, we spoke only Spanish, where my mother frequently said I talked *como una cotorra*, like a parrot. I was very verbal, very outspoken, and as I got older, *Mami* used to say that I should become a lawyer because I always wanted the last word. In school, on the other hand, I was mute, at least for the first few months of my education. By the end of that year, besides learning enough English to get along, as well as the rudiments of reading, I learned other valuable lessons: I learned that reading would open up the world to me, that learning was exciting, and that education was my best hope for a better life. There were other less sanguine lessons as well: I learned that to be Puerto Rican was at best an inconvenience, and at worst a handicap. I learned that English was the language of value and that, although Spanish was the language of family and love and nurturing, it was also a language that had low status. I learned that, as one teacher told me, it was "rude to speak Spanish in class." Most of all, I learned that school was where you learned things that were worthwhile and consequential, and that home was where you learned things that you never disclosed in school. There was, in effect, a tremendous wall between home and school, and that wall was to remain intact until I became a teacher myself and I began to question why this should be so.

LEARNING ENGLISH—WITH AND WITHOUT HELP

My sister Lydia, a year older than me and in 2nd grade, was already in her 3rd year of school because she had been fortunate enough to attend kindergarten. But because we lived in a fifth-floor, walk-up tenement apartment and because we had a 3-year-old brother, Freddy, who, it was already clear, was not like other children (years later, he would be diagnosed as developmentally disabled and autistic) and could not be left alone, I couldn't attend kindergarten. It would have been impossible for my mother to bring Freddy along while taking me to kindergarten and my sister to 2nd grade, then return for me at noon, and finally pick Lydia up at 3:00. I missed out on kindergarten—I had been looking forward to it because I saw Lydia come home with pretty art projects—but luckily my sister taught me English as she learned it. Unlike me, Lydia has some fond memories of her early schooling because she met Miss Powell, a teacher who took her out of her classroom and helped her learn English.

It must have been 1949 or so, and the Puerto Rican community in New York City was exploding. Because of this, the field of English as a second language (ESL) was just beginning to take hold. Miss Powell was among the early ESL specialists and she made a deep impression, according to a poem Lydia wrote years later, just a brief part of which follows:

I Remember

I remember kindergarten
I remember having to say good-bye to Mami
I remember crying
I remember not understanding the teacher
I remember the English lessons with pretty Miss Powell
Who made the boxy words fit just right in my mouth without
        pain . . . (Cortés, 2000)

By the time I hit 1st grade, Miss Powell was no longer around and I was left to fend for myself.

In spite of how much she may have taught me, Lydia could not have prepared me for all the contingencies of 1st grade, including how to ask my teacher for help in tying a hat. My classroom teacher, whose name I do not recall, must not have had an easy time of it. Ours was a school of immigrants and home-grown "minorities": The newly arriving Puerto Ricans were mixed in with other Caribbeans and African Americans, along with older settlements of Russian, Polish, Ukrainian, Italian, and other European immigrants. Although most of the children of European immigrants had more English than we did, still the classroom was no doubt a challenging place, not unlike contemporary classrooms in many cities and, increasingly, suburbs too. This is why I frequently remind people that diversity—cultural, racial, and linguistic—is nothing new in the United States: Sixty years ago, in my school, you could find children from various continents and nations who spoke numerous languages and who reflected different values, lifestyles, and histories. Cultural diversity is, and has always been, part of our historic legacy.

I do not remember how long it took me to feel comfortable in English. I suppose that with the help of my sister and classmates, I was able to learn quite quickly. I was a "good girl," quiet and compliant throughout my schooling, and I was often the "teacher's pet." As soon as I learned to decipher text, reading became my escape. Another fixed memory: I am sitting on a step in the concrete schoolyard and as my classmates are running around playing tag and other games at recess, I am rushing to finish the pages in my workbook. It seems I preferred reading to playing. I learned to love school, and I also loved to read. Well, to say that I loved to read is an understatement. I devoured books. Although we didn't have books at home and bedtime stories were never a family tradition, as we got older, my mother brought us to the public library once a month. There, I checked out six books, the maximum allowed, and savored each one, a delicious meal for a hungry child.

REJECTING SPANISH AND ALL THINGS PUERTO RICAN

As we got older, Lydia and I took to speaking English more than Spanish, especially with each other. It was easier to do so: Not only was it the language of school and of radio (no television for us until we were teenagers) but it was also, we already sensed, the language of status and power. Speaking Spanish became a private thing, something we did, if we had to, only at home. So, while our parents continued, stubbornly, to speak to us in Spanish, we took to answering them in English, wanting desperately to fit in with *los americanos* by sounding and acting like them. By the time we were in junior high school, we studiously avoided Spanish music as well, and we yearned for "American" food. In the process, we learned to feel ashamed of our parents, our extended family, and our community. It is not unlike the kind of pressure many young people face today.

We wanted, for example, to eat like Americans. Lydia and I were both quite skinny. I recall my sister's 5th-grade teacher, Mr. Seidman, a caring and committed teacher who was no doubt concerned that we were not getting enough to eat, or that what we were eating was not healthy. Mr. Seidman probably reasoned that as poor immigrants, we had little food in the house. In his well-meaning way, he spoke to *Mami* about good nutrition and he suggested that *Mami* feed us different kinds of food, healthier options than we were eating (although I doubt that he knew anything about our diet). I do not know if he ever showed her the "Seven Basic Foods" chart that, along with the ubiquitous Palmer Method handwriting chart and American flag, graced every classroom wall in the school. I do remember, though, feeling ashamed that none of the foods we ate at home had made their way onto that chart. No rice, no Puerto Rican beans, no *plátanos*, no *cocos*, no *guayabas*; in fact, almost everything on that chart was unrecognizable. No wonder, then, that I thought we would surely die of malnutrition!

We may have been poor, but in our home, there was never a shortage of good nutritious food. After all, by this time, our father owned a *bodega*, a Latin American grocery store that catered to the growing Puerto Rican population in our Brooklyn neighborhood. It was a tiny place, a basement apartment converted into a store where both my parents worked many hours a day, my father 14 or 16 and my mother 6 or 8, with Freddy in tow, leaving only to go home to prepare dinner. At home, we ate rice and beans nearly every day, along with *plátanos* and chicken or meat, and salads of lettuce, tomatoes, avocados, and other vegetables. For breakfast, we had what we were later to call "baby coffee," that is, a shot of coffee in a glass of sweetened milk, along with *pan con mantequilla*, toasted bread. At night, we had *ponche* made with warm milk, egg, sugar, and vanilla, and for a treat, we drank malta, a nonalcoholic very sweet thick malt.

But when we started school and saw and heard about "American food," we immediately coveted it. We would beg *Mami* to make hamburgers and hot dogs and other foods that we instinctively sensed had more caché than our Puerto Rican food. *Mami* would just smile and keep cooking whatever it was that she was making. At the same time, Lydia and I developed a taste for the foods of our immigrant neighborhood, learning to love the knishes and fat juicy pickles we picked from the barrel in our local Jewish deli, as well as Italian pasta and the newest sensation in our 1950s neighborhood, pizza. Developing these new tastes expanded our world, and yet somehow our own Puerto Rican food took second place in the same way that our language, culture, and community connections were becoming weaker. This is one of the consequences of growing up without bilingual education, something that I was to realize only years later when I became a bilingual teacher.

Although I don't remember exactly when I became biliterate, I think it was sometime early in my life. Clearly, I never studied Spanish grammar, reading, or writing as a child, but because I was a strong reader and a good student, I suppose that my literacy skills in English transferred over. I do remember that one year when Lydia and I spent a summer in Puerto Rico with relatives, I was able to read the few postcards that my parents sent. *Mami* usually wrote to us in English but *Papi*, with his 4th-grade education, preferred Spanish, and I was able to decipher his messages. I was 11 years old.

CHANGING VENUES

By the time I was 13, we had moved from the ghetto to a more middle-class neighborhood in Brooklyn. I began attending a junior high school where I was, I think, the only Puerto Rican. The transition was a difficult one, both because the school's academic standards were far more rigorous than those of my former schools, and also because I felt lonely (my sister, by this time, was in high school). My grades, which had been the highest in my classes in my ghetto schools, at first plummeted; it took a few months for me to raise them once again and to begin to feel more comfortable in this new environment.

My classmates were Jewish and Italian, but they were not immigrants. Instead, they were 2nd, 3rd, and even 4th generation, and very assimilated to U.S. life. Even though I never quite felt at home in my new junior high and, later, at Erasmus Hall High School, a highly regarded public school in my new neighborhood, I am forever grateful that I was given the opportunity to attend those schools. I am fairly certain that had I remained in the schools in my previous neighborhood, it was unlikely that I would have gone to college. College was not an option in the ghetto schools I attended; it was hardly even mentioned. At Erasmus Hall High School, however, it was taken for granted that nearly everyone would go to college.

In junior high and high school, I decided not to take Spanish, not because I was ashamed of speaking Spanish but because I was fairly fluent in it and wanted to experience another language. I took French and I excelled in it; it became my strongest subject, something that even then I realized was because I already spoke Spanish. When I got to college, I decided to take Spanish, and it was there that I really developed my biliteracy. In fact, I decided to minor in Spanish, while majoring in elementary education, my lifelong goal to become a teacher having been cemented when I was just a child.

COLLEGE AND BEYOND: RECALCULATING IDENTITIES

Lydia and I both attended college. Although we stayed in Brooklyn and commuted to St. John's University every day, the experience was a life-changing one. I wanted very much to fit in, and in a college community where there were just three Puerto Ricans (my sister and I were two of them), this was not always easy. At St. John's, I changed my name from Sonia to "Sunny," not just because it sounded more American, but also because I thought it better reflected my personality. Although we had many friends and college was generally an expanding and positive experience, there were some moments that made clear to us that we were still outsiders. I remember, for example, the night that a couple of our friends came over to the house as we prepared to go to a party. One of the girls had gone overboard in applying her make-up and as she took a look at herself in the mirror, she said, "Oh, my God! I look like a Puerto Rican!" She quickly realized what she had said and added, "Oh, I don't mean the two of you," something that Lydia and I heard repeatedly—and sometimes still hear—when people wanted to distance us from other Puerto Ricans.

For the first time in my life, I had Latino teachers. I loved my Spanish classes, and I remember some of my teachers very fondly—a Spanish woman, and a Cuban man, among others. It was an eye-opener for me to see Latino professionals in the classroom. True, I had a couple of cousins who had arrived from Puerto Rico after high school to attend college in New York, later becoming social workers, but they were definitely the exception in our family of factory, service, and blue collar workers. Seeing Latino professors strengthened my resolve to become a teacher and may even have planted the seed that in the future I too could become a university professor.

Not only did I minor in Spanish, but I also joined the Spanish Club and I became its president in my junior year. Just like a GPS device when you take a wrong turn ("recalculating," it says), I too was "recalculating" my identity through these experiences. I was beginning to understand that speaking Spanish, rather than being a burden, could be a tremendous advantage. I decided that after college I would attend New York University's graduate program in Spain (the only country I knew of where such programs existed) to study for my master's degree in Spanish and Latin American literature. Ironically, it was this experience that brought me back full circle to my language and my culture. In Spain, I was seen not only as worthwhile but even as special because I was Puerto Rican and spoke some Spanish. This was a shock to me, but a great relief as well. It was the first time I had felt affirmed for being who I was rather than for hiding my identity. In the interest of full disclosure, I should also mention that it was at this point that I met and fell madly in love with my husband-to-be (still madly in love and still my husband after 43 years), which I am certain made my experience in Spain even more wonderful.

I worked on retrieving more of my Spanish and I learned about the magnificent literature of many Spanish-speaking nations. I relearned some of the things I had chosen to bury, not only some of the Spanish I had discarded but also the traditions and values that I had neglected. I returned a year later to begin my teaching career with a new and more positive perspective on my identity and my community. I dropped "Sunny" and became "Sonia" again.

TEACHING AND LEARNING

My first teaching position was in an intermediate school in Brooklyn, where I taught English, Spanish, French, and, ironically, NE (or non-English, as the English language learners were called at the time), teaching children who were not unlike who I had been just a few years earlier. But a couple of years later when a call went out to interview for an experimental elementary school that was to be called simply P.S. 25: The Bilingual School, I quickly applied. Housed in a nearly century-old school in the South Bronx—a largely Puerto Rican community—the school would be the first bilingual school in the Northeast and only the second in the nation. Supported by a progressive superintendent, the school was established as the result of a long struggle and advocacy on the part of Puerto Rican and other community activists for an education that would affirm students' identities at the same time that it provided them with a high-quality education.

I was interviewed by Hernán LaFontaine, a young principal, who a few years later would gain recognition as the first Director of the Office of Bilingual Education in New York City, and later as Director of the Office of Bilingual Education for the federal government, among other impressive accomplishments. During the interview, he explained that P.S. 25 was to be founded on two major premises: the value of bilingualism and the importance of parent involvement. I don't know why he hired me because, frankly, as I told him, I had misgivings, or at least questions, about both of these. After all, I had done pretty well without a bilingual education, hadn't I? And in terms of parent involvement, although my parents were firm believers in the power of education, they had been reluctant to even enter school buildings, much less take an active role in our schools. I thought, wouldn't active and demanding parents simply create more problems for teachers?

My misgivings about bilingual education, I think, were the result of my own experience as a student, and of my having bought into the U.S. hegemonic ideology that resists, or even directly prohibits, the use of languages other than English in society in general, and certainly in schools in particular. At the time, I guess I hadn't quite thought through the contradictions about language that I saw around me: Why, for example, were monolingual English speakers encouraged to study another language in high school and college, even though most of them would never truly learn it, at the same time that native speakers of other languages were pressured to forget their native language and become monolingual English speakers? And why was it viewed as a tremendous achievement when monolingual English speakers became fluent in a second language, while native speakers of other languages who learned English were never afforded the same level of respect? These were questions I suppose I had never really grappled with, and so the thought that a public school founded on the philosophy of equal respect for two languages and cultures was foreign to me.

Hernán hired me anyway. P.S. 25 would forever change how I viewed teaching, bilingualism, and the role of families in education. Within a couple of months, I was convinced of the wisdom of both bilingual education and parent involvement because I experienced firsthand the tremendous difference that they made in the lives of children, teachers, and families, and even in the larger community. In college I had been trained to "not smile until Christmas," and to "leave your cultural baggage outside." My professors emphasized that my major role as a teacher was to "assimilate" my students into the mainstream, among other myths of teacher lore. Yet, at P.S. 25, I learned just the opposite: I learned the value of beginning to establish close and caring relationships with my students and their families immediately, from the very first day; I learned the value of bringing my entire self into my teaching, and to share my life with my students; and I learned that assimilation can be harmful to students' learning, their feelings about themselves, and their connection with their communities.

STARTING WHERE WE'RE AT

In college, I had also been taught to "start where the kids are at," the best advice I learned through my entire teacher education program. But to "start where the kids are at" you need to *know* where they're at, and the only way to do that is to become a student of your students. As a Puerto Rican, I had a leg up, of course, because many of my students were Puerto Rican, but still I had a lot to learn about *these* particular children in *this* particular community. I had to learn what their lives were like, who loved them, and what their dreams were. I had to learn who their families were and what they wanted for their children. So, as I visited them in their apartments and they visited me in my classroom, I got to know the families, and together we learned about one another.

P.S. 25 was a wonderful place. Although only about a third of the teachers were Latinos, everyone in the school was bilingual, from the principal to the janitorial staff. The students were primarily Latinos (about 85%), but everyone was expected to become bilingual. I was a 4th-grade teacher and I taught my students all their content, some in English and some in Spanish. I loved my students and I loved teaching them in both languages, just as I loved learning about Puerto Rican history—something

I had never learned in school—right along with my students. At the same time, I sensed that learning only about one's own culture was not enough, and I attempted to create a multicultural curriculum (although in the late 1960s we did not yet use this language) through which my students would learn to value all people. Students were free to communicate in either language, and their families were welcome everywhere in the school, from our classrooms to the parent room next to the principal's office.

Of course, P.S. 25 was not without its challenges. Because bilingual education was in its infancy, there were few materials that were appropriate for our students. Most of the books we were able to find were published in Spain and Mexico, with a few from Puerto Rico, but the palm trees, coconuts, flamenco dancers, bull fights, and other themes and illustrations in those books were far removed from the lives of our urban students in the Northeast United States. We spent countless hours creating our own curriculum and most mornings copying things on the solitary mimeograph machine in the main office. Being a poor school, we had to become resourceful about how to use the community and the city as our curriculum. It was also hard to find teachers who could teach in this school. In fact, until I went to P.S. 25, I was convinced that I was the only Puerto Rican or Latina teacher in the entire New York City Public School system of over 55,000 teachers, but while I was happy to find others at the school, we were still few and far between in the late 1960s. But in spite of all the challenges, P.S. 25 was an exciting, energizing, and transformative place: It changed my mind about the role of language and culture in learning, and it became the basis for much of my professional work that was to follow. Most of all, it helped me learn to be proud not only of my background but, more important, of my parents, my language, and my community.

CREATING A NEW IDENTITY

Just as with my students, I also had to "start where I was at." I had begun my life as a monolingual speaker of Spanish who lived in a traditional Puerto Rican family, albeit transposed to New York City and translated in a different context. I had to learn to respect who I was, who my parents were, and what they spoke, said, and believed. But I also had to create my own identity. I could not be a Puerto Rican of my parents' generation, nor could I be completely American with no vestiges of my background and upbringing. It has been a long process, and P.S. 25 helped me do these things.

Although I could not benefit from bilingual education as a young child, I was able to benefit from it as a teacher. Now, many years after I learned how to tie a bow, I am so grateful to my parents for giving me the gift of language and culture, a gift that I have passed on to my daughters. My parents held onto their identities and, by doing so, they helped me to forge my own, an identity different from theirs, one that is part U.S., part Puerto Rican, part "Nuyorican," a hybrid identity forged in love and in struggle. They helped me become bilingual and biliterate against the odds.

CHAPTER 2

Words Were All We Had:
Reflections on Becoming Biliterate

Josué M. González

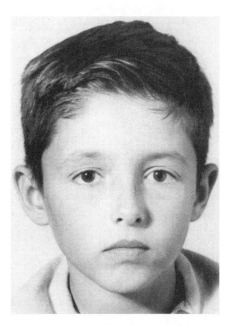

Josué González's educational and literacy journey began in the Rio Grande Valley of Texas where Spanish played an essential role in everyday life, and where Chicanos constituted a numerical majority. As a student, Josué was surrounded by role models from his own cultural community—a testament that they were a vital part of the social fabric of society. In these sociocultural contexts where individuals are immersed in a strong bilingual, biliterate community, speaking Spanish is a given, bilingualism is the norm, and biliteracy is a likely by-product. This chapter suggests that when a community, or school, allows the languages of its members to co-exist and thrive without threat to either linguistic community, and without unfounded suppositions that native languages interfere with learning, students are more likely to become bilingual and biliterate. (Note: The title of this chapter inspired the title for the book as the phrase, "words were all we had," aptly captures the most important source of knowledge that these authors brought to school.)

My first words and thousands more for years to come were all in Spanish. While I was born in the United States, as were my parents, the corner of Texas where I first attempted to speak was not fully connected, culturally, to the rest of the country. It was a remnant of a different era. That corner of the Texas/Mexico border has never had an English name, and it has been home to Spanish-speaking people since the 1700s. Of course, they were called Spaniards then rather than Hispanics or Latinos. Most of Texas, at that time, was part of the *Provincia del Nuevo Santander*, not the United States. My own family roots in the soil of south Texas go back far enough to include the awarding, by the Spanish crown, of a sizable portion of land to an ancestor of mine. I say this in the interest of full disclosure. I acknowledge, of course, those lands belonged to peoples who were there long before my Spanish-speaking ancestors arrived.

Speaking Spanish before English was one of those decisions I did not make. That was due to the home and community environment in which I was born and raised. I cannot remember anyone who worried about the fact that we spoke one language and the rest of the country spoke another. Further, the responsibility for harmonizing this difference was never mentioned. The schools played a role, of course. Other than Spanish courses, classes were conducted entirely in English, but the teachers in our community were all bilingual and few of them seemed to worry about our tight embrace of Spanish. Someday, somehow, this would work itself out.

MY HOME AND MY COMMUNITY

Nearly everyone in our border town was poor. Perhaps we imagined that words were all we had, and we were not about to give any of them up. The absence of English outside the classroom was not regarded as a problem or an impediment to upward mobility. Living in a dirt-poor border community was, most certainly, an impediment to upward mobility, but no one that I can remember blamed it on language. My family was school conscious and education oriented. My parents spoke often to my sisters and me about the importance of doing well in our studies. Reading instruction, in Spanish, began early. There were two reasons for this. First, my parents wanted us to be literate because they read Spanish and wanted their children to keep that skill alive. Just as important, they wanted us to participate actively in religious activities, and we could not do that without being able to read. Looking back now, I cannot say with certainty which of the two reasons was the more important. Nor was there any focus on the method used to teach us how to read. We learned to read by reading.

The first reference book I ever knew was a Bible Concordance, a huge cross-referencing index that showed where in the Bible particular topics were mentioned. My father, a lay Methodist minister, loved that book. It contained information, and its regular use made him more adept at citing Biblical references in his sermons. At around 4th grade I experienced the arrival of another reference book in our school, the *Encyclopedia Britannica*. I was blown away by its contents, its imposing presence, and even its smell. I longed to be kept in after school so I could wallow in it and inhale the intoxicating aroma of its newness. One of my teachers pointed out that the complete set cost several hundred dollars. She encouraged us to wash our hands before using the encyclopedia to avoid smudging the beautiful pages with our untidy hands. Most of us were not willing to go that far.

I have always wondered whether other kids were as enthralled as I was by the smell of new books, especially a whole stack of 20 large volumes. I confess that, even today, when a new book arrives in the mail, I open the package with anticipation of the smell held captive within. Because I was too well behaved, I was never detained after school to fulfill my yearnings toward the *Encyclopedia Britannica*. I could only steal periodic glimpses and quick sniffs into its pages. As far as I knew then encyclopedias came only in English, a fact that did not deter me from trying to read it.

The first narrative book read to me was *Genoveva de Brabante*. I remember that my grandmother would retrieve it furtively and only when no one else was around. She would sit in her rocking chair and read to me, always stopping at a particularly interesting point in the story that left me clamoring for more. The book in question was the equivalent of a modern-day romance novel. Judging by Internet traffic on blogs dealing with Spanish literature, there were many children in Spain and Latin America who had this book read to them.

The mythical Genoveva was a virtuous and beautiful young girl who lived in Spain in the mid-13th century. At a young age she married a dashing young man who promptly went off to war leaving her in the care of his relatives. An evil satyr of a relative pursued the young woman but failed to lure her into his bed. The man became incensed and in retaliation accused her of infidelity. Genoveva was sentenced to die. Because of her beauty and virtue, no one wanted to act as executioner. So Genoveva was simply left in the middle of the forest to be eaten alive by wild animals. None of the animals appeared to be interested in a free lunch so Genoveva survived. Eventually, her husband discovered her and realized her innocence; he took her back home where they lived happily ever after. I have never actually seen a copy of the book other than my grandmother's well-worn copy with its tattered cover. It was not a story written for boys. But it was a moment of closeness between my grandmother and me that I appreciated.

READING ENGLISH

Learning to read in English was much more trying than learning to read in Spanish. I learned to read English through a state-adopted series of basal books called *Fun with Dick and Jane*. In these books, a nuclear family of father, mother, sister, brother, dog, and cat said inane things to one another, such as, "Look look, Jane. See Spot run. Come Spot come." Until 3rd grade or so, there was no plot and no apparent reason for the repetitive language. *Fun with Dick and Jane* left almost no impression at all except one of ennui. *La bella* Genoveva was infinitely more interesting.

BILINGUAL PRIDE

Some of the most positive and most negative aspects of my relationship to, and with, Spanish occurred in my high school years. I was a fairly good student, especially in English and Spanish. I managed to graduate in the top 10% of my class. My only problem was in a subject I no longer recall and with a teacher that does not deserve to be remembered. Mr. Pérez, like most of my other teachers, was Hispanic although he did not wear that skin comfortably. He never spoke Spanish to students or other teachers. The other teachers spoke English to students in and out of class. If, however, they wished to communicate something outside their teacher role, they would, on occasion, switch into Spanish. Although exchanges were generally brief, students considered it important that they would choose to speak Spanish, the language of our parents and grandparents. It was as if they meant to be more familial or intimate with us. It was a small example of how my school community adapted, respectfully, to the social variations of language. I cannot say how this communicative concept first developed but it was useful because we tended to listen more carefully, *con las dos orejas* (with two ears), as someone said. Mr. Pérez, however, did not participate in these brief diglossic episodes. To us the man was an odd bird, one we were quite unaccustomed to and who exceeded our understanding of "identity issues," as we later learned such things were called.

Mr. Pérez sticks in my memory for an episode related to Spanish. He was the faculty sponsor of the National Honor Society (NHS), a well-behaved, high-achieving group in whose company I fitted in only with difficulty. Culturally, I was more attracted to the *campesino* kids, the farm workers who left school early in the spring and did not return until the fall, after they had picked all the crops up north. These well-traveled kids were more interesting than the members of the NHS who attended school every day, did their homework with religious zeal, and were given extra school duties because they seemed to enjoy doing chores for teachers.

But I digress. One day, at one of the sleepy noontime meetings, Mr. Pérez proposed that the NHS should adopt the practice of speaking only English in school. About half of the group nodded their approval albeit unenthusiastically. For reasons that I did not fully understand at the time, I rose to speak against the sponsor's proposal. I no longer remember the exact words I used, but they had to do with the symbolic rejection of our parents' language and of the historic culture of which it was a part, and so on. Mr. Pérez did not react well to my dissent. He interrupted my speech, jumped to his feet, and loudly repeated his argument, his face growing redder by the second.

"Déjalo que hable" (let him speak), said one of my friends, objecting to the interruption of my response. For a full half minute there was total silence as Mr. Pérez sat back down, silenced by a student. At that precise moment a bell rang, ending the meeting without a vote on the teacher's motion. It was never brought back for reconsideration and Mr. Pérez never spoke to me again. This was offset by my classmates' smiles of appreciation. *"Dale gas,"* one of them said, a vernacular form of encouragement roughly equivalent to "Right on!" To further situate this episode, I point out that it occurred sometime in the late 1950s. At that point the issue was not one of struggling against oppressive language policies. None of us were there yet. The important point was that no one in my part of the country had ever heard of resisting a teacher's control of a student organization or of a student asking a teacher to be quiet. For me, a small seed had been planted that would germinate for several years and become the basis of my advocacy for bilingual education. The civil rights era was around the corner and I was unknowingly preparing for it.

In high school, Sofía Méndez had a greater effect on me than Mr. Pérez or the NHS. My first puppy love affair played out almost totally in Spanish. Sofía was a grade ahead of me. She was a farm worker kid. Every year she and her family would stretch a tarp across the top of a truck, crawl in, and drive for days to the cotton fields of West Texas or the sugar beet fields of Michigan. To me, Sofía was an exotic creature. She had long beautiful flaming red hair and beautiful smiling eyes that were rarely sad. She could tease me mercilessly by simply looking at me and smiling. Sofía and I shared an odd lunch period with a few other students whose schedules had also been somehow mangled. She and I got into the habit of sitting under a particular tree on the school grounds and having wonderful conversations on a variety of subjects. It became our private place, a wonderful noontime interlude in which two teenagers met to have unscripted conversations on many subjects.

Sofía was a lover of the Spanish language. If I were late for our meetings I would find her reading Mexican *novelas* of the type that are illustrated with comic-strip illustrations in black and white. The stories always included unrequited love, betrayal, and tears. She read using only her right eye because her long hair always covered the left half of her face. She did this to hide an ugly scar that marred her cheek. She never told me how she got it. Sofía read fast. She raced through the Spanish pulp fiction faster than anything she could do in English, a subject in which she was mediocre. Oddly, she had never taken a Spanish course or studied the language formally.

"I love Spanish," she told me, "I think it's the language of the gods."

"Really? Who told you that? How do you know what language God speaks?" I probably smirked as I asked the question because I remember her slapping my knee with her *novela* for having dared to ask. "How do you know he didn't speak English?"

"No seas tonto" ("Don't be a dummy!"), she said. "Spanish comes from the Mediterranean, and the Holy Land is at the other end of that. Besides, English didn't even exist at that time. He had to preach in many languages. Doesn't it make sense that Jesus went there and learned to speak Spanish?"

I wanted to please her so I made it a point to speak more Spanish than English to her. Sofía was never my girlfriend nor did our friendship ever go beyond our noontime conversations. In early April, she told me her family was ready to go north to work. Next week, she said, she would be dropping out of school but would come back in the fall.

"You be a good boy until I get back, OK?" I promised her I would be, but I never saw her again. Through the high school grapevine I learned she had married and would not be coming back to school. I blamed the vapid pulp novels for her marriage. That weekend I learned a new *ranchera* song on the guitar. My favorite line in the song said *"la distancia entre los dos es cada día más grande"* ("the distance between us grows longer each day"). I sang it endlessly until friends and family alike suggested, strongly, that I learn a new song.

High school was also memorable for the Spanish play, a yearly theatrical production put on by students in the advanced Spanish classes. Usually a comedy, the Spanish play was a highlight for students and the community. We rehearsed with gusto, making up for any lack of acting skills with exaggerated mugging. To be selected for the cast was a badge of honor among Spanish students. I was in the Spanish play for 2 of my 4 years in high school and the memories of the plays are still vivid. Our version of *Charlie's Aunt* (*La Tía de Carlos*) brought down the house every performance. For several weeks I flirted with pursuing an acting career. When I mentioned this to the counselor, I received a cold blank stare that caused me to never mention the subject again.

I cannot end my reflections on high school without trying to explain a difficult memory of another teacher, Mrs. Archuleta. Diane Archuleta was a bright young woman, perfectly fluent in both languages. She came up with the idea of creating the equivalent of an AP English class for some of the seniors who might be college bound. To avoid conflicts with our other classes, the Oxford English class, as it came to be known by the other students, was held at 7:00 a.m., a truly bad hour for a teenage boy but especially bad because of the high requirements of the class. Mrs. Archuleta essentially taught the freshman English composition course at a university level. No. Actually, she exceeded the requirements of that course in most universities. Daily for an entire year, the sleepy-headed group of students, most of them native speakers of Spanish, wrote a 5-page paper, on many subjects, which we submitted at the end of the class. Mrs. Archuleta would mark up the papers and return them the next day liberally sprinkled with red marks. In the exaggerated sentimentalism of teenagers, I thought of my papers as being soaked in blood.

Few other teachers in that school, or any other, could have possibly extracted that much work from us for a full year. But no one objected and almost everyone stayed awake. Our teacher explained that this discipline was a bit like a stinky vitamin drink. It was a bit unpleasant going down but good for our long-term academic health. It proved to be that, of course. Years later, after publishing my first article in an academic journal, I received a letter from Mrs. Archuleta. It read in part, "Dear Josué, I have just finished reading your article in the X journal." My blood ran cold. I could not believe that my English teacher had read the first article I had ever published. To my relief, she went on to say that she had enjoyed it and wished me much luck in my career. This teacher still haunts me. She is only 5 or 6 years older than I. Given her interest in former students and their writing, she may very well be reading this piece too.

Mrs. Archuleta influenced my relationship to the English language in at least two ways. First, I still find it easier to write early in the morning with the assist of a fresh pot of coffee. Second, I write, rewrite, and edit numerous times, an easy connection to her pleas that we always seek to improve our writing by cleaning up after ourselves.

COLLEGE YEARS

Like most young people from poor schools, I received little guidance in preparing for college, choosing a course of study, or deciding on a career. I attended a small public university in South Texas where Latinos, at the time, constituted about 10% of the student population. The university offered highly respected degrees in animal husbandry and natural gas engineering, neither of which was of interest to me. Instead, I wandered into the university as a freshman thinking of majoring in journalism because Mrs. Archuleta had told me I showed promise as a writer. I found that the department of journalism was small and uninspiring, too technical and uninteresting in terms of the work expected of students. I rejected journalism and moved on to a second choice, English. I considered an English major because of a parallel interest in English history, along with studying the history and literature of Spain and Latin America, which I had begun to do early on. It was my first formal connecting of the two languages; a formalizing of my interest in biliteracy. But, English was too uninspiring and the writing exercises unchallenging. I finally settled on a Spanish major. I read Spanish and Latin American authors and poets avidly. I discovered Pablo Neruda and went on, later, to write a master's thesis on his poetry long before the rest of the world took note of him. Today the various "generations" of poets blend into one long undifferentiated poem. But, as an undergraduate I was clear on every poetic movement, who was in it, and what each had contributed. I appreciated the elegance of the language used in ways I had never before imagined. I memorized poems that I then recited to friends. At beer parties I could easily be coaxed into reciting *El Día Que Me Quieras* or *El Brindis del Bohemio*, or *Canto a América*. I was clearly enjoying the social aspects of Spanish more than my peers were. I could not know, then, how that enjoyment would influence my career in education.

My exuberant interest in Spanish and Spanish American literature came to the attention of the chairman of the Department of Foreign Languages. (At that time no one gave a second thought to the possibility that Spanish someday would cease to be considered a "foreign" tongue in the United States.) Don Pedro Ortíz was an easy-going gregarious gentleman from San Sebastian, Spain. He was the only man on campus who wore a beret and a goatee. More important, he reveled in the company of students. A bachelor, he enjoyed having students visit him at home to listen to classical music, of which he had an enormous collection. He could also be counted on to have a good collection of red wines, which young people from South Texas knew nothing about although we were eager to learn. Don Pedro offered me my first job in higher education: to become his grader. I was responsible chiefly for a correspondence course in Spanish culture and civilization with half a dozen students. I accepted the job with pride. Some student papers were in English; some in Spanish. This required me to polish my grammar in order to grade the papers properly. I spent many hours either preparing for these tasks or carrying them out, and my Spanish improved a great deal. My mentor spent little time mentoring me but his wine cabinet and his exquisite high-fidelity music system were always available. The next year Don Pedro gave me a second job managing the language lab and helping students with their grammar and conjugation problems in Spanish. Without ceremony, a career as a teacher of Spanish was launched.

BILINGUAL EDUCATION ARRIVES

As I was completing my master's degree a few years later, I tried to locate Don Pedro to get his advice on this career move. I discovered that he had been killed by a truck while taking photographs of wildflowers by the side of the road. How like you, I thought, to be killed over a frigging flower! I was momentarily more angry than sad.

When I heard of a job opening in a nearby town specifically in the new field of bilingual education, I applied. I was turned down for lack of experience. No one that I knew had done bilingual education in South Texas for the past century so who could possibly be experienced? The hiring decision was in the hands of monolingual school administrators, which, I assumed, was the reason they would overlook me as a valued staff member.

To work in bilingual education I found it necessary to move to Austin where a special project to develop bilingual curriculum materials was underway. I received a much warmer welcome there when the people in charge, who were also monolingual English speakers, found that I was literate in Spanish. They had realized relatively late in planning the project that people with language skills in two languages would be needed in bilingual education. A bonus in my move to Austin was my taking a course at the University of Texas with the iconic professor, George I. Sánchez, perhaps the first academic to promote the idea that Mexican American students should be taught in Spanish first. He had been proposing this since 1935. Now, he was an angry old man who assumed his ideas had been rejected, that no one had listened. He now referred to everyone in the education establishment as *una bola de pendejos,* a major vulgarity.

BILINGUAL ACTIVISM

There is little doubt that joining the bilingual education movement that began in the mid-1960s had a dramatic impact on my relationship to, and with, my two languages. Previously, I had taken them both for granted as sources of education and enjoyment. Now they became the direct objects of professional concern, headaches, achievements, and disappointments. The element of fun that had characterized my childhood and youth with respect to biliteracy, poems, novels, and dreams of European travel evaporated. Headaches and disappointments took over at least temporarily. I realized that there was another side to languages: that they could be used to oppress or liberate. That in the case of Latinos, we had been slow to recognize this and act accordingly. The future of Spanish in the United States was uncertain. I could now see that it was the most important form of cultural expression of Latinos and it was seriously threatened by nativists' attitudes. I worked to keep the spirit and the language alive and thriving until the demographics of Latinos could catch up politically. In November 1973, I gave a talk in Albuquerque, New Mexico, in which I said that we needed to hang on tenaciously to our language at least until the year 2000. After that, the sheer mass of the Latino population would ensure the survival of the language. I believe that has now happened.

CHAPTER 3

A Lifelong Quest for Biliteracy: A Personal and Professional Journey

Carmen I. Mercado

Although born in Puerto Rico, Carmen Mercado attended schools in East Harlem and finally in Queens, where she graduated from high school. Early on, she identified with her native language, referring to herself as "Spanish." Beginning in junior high school, she spent summers in Puerto Rico where she gained a better understanding of herself as Puerto Rican, and an awareness of how her Spanish language variety was disparaged. These experiences served as strong motivation to attain an academic and professional level of Spanish commensurate with her English skills. With strong conviction of the worth of her goal, Carmen set out in pursuit of this goal, sparing no opportunity to enhance her Spanish. Carmen's chapter reveals the various strategies she used (and continues to use) to attain her goal; it provides bilingual teachers with a model to emulate.

I am what Guadalupe Valdés refers to as a circumstantial bilingual and what I prefer to describe as an emergent biliterate professional. For the past 3 decades, I have persisted in a struggle to attain a level of competence in reading, writing, and speaking in Spanish commensurate with my role as a practitioner-scholar, at a level comparable to my competence in English. Some theorize that being equally competent in two languages is a practical impossibility. I remain unconvinced and pretend that I can achieve this. Powerful technological tools and the mass media of our 21st century put the Spanish-speaking word and worlds at my fingertips. Fast-paced travel drops me into these different worlds in a few short hours. All these tools and resources have enabled me to develop and extend basic communicative competencies. They do so, despite little formal study and the dominance of English in the professional (and social) milieus I navigate as a Puerto Rican in New York.

THE EARLY YEARS

"I'm Spanish," was my automatic response growing up in New York City in the 1950s and 1960s. This is how I explained why my name and my upbringing were different from those of my classmates. Spanish, the language of my family and heritage, has formed part of how I have chosen to define myself even though I have lived in New York City most of my life. It has shaped and defined me in ways I still don't fully understand. As the title of Norma González's (2001) book proclaims, "I am my language."

I was born on the island of Puerto Rico in Toa Baja, a sugar-growing region on the northeast coast, east of San Juan. As a result of U.S. policies, the area, along with the rest of the island, was transformed dramatically by a shift from an agrarian to a manufacturing economy. This shift left many workers displaced, my father among them, which is why he ventured north, with his brother's assistance, to try a job at Silvercup (a large commercial bakery at the foot of the Queensboro Bridge, connecting Queens and Manhattan). A year or so later, he returned to New York with my mother and his two young children. We made history as part of one of largest airborne migrations to settle in East Harlem (or El Barrio) in the 1950s. I consider it significant that my parents were mature adults in their mid-30s when they settled in New York. They had completed an 8th-grade education in Puerto Rico, at the time the equivalent of a high school diploma. Required to study English, they arrived in New York with sufficient competence in the language to meet their needs. I surmise this from the stories they told me, but Spanish remained the language of the home throughout their lifetime. Our apartment was a hub of activity with a constant flow of visitors and short-term guests (*bordantes*), rituals and celebrations, music and dancing. I now appreciate traces of literacy that were unremarkable to me growing up, such as fragments of lengthy letters mom exchanged regularly with her sisters in Puerto Rico, a common practice among women pioneers.

As the growing Puerto Rican community gradually infringed territory staked out by the Italians, one of the largest immigrant communities in the nation, occasional clashes robbed us of friends and relatives, but never our humanity. My parents bridged differences and sustained cordial relationships with Italian neighbors, who offered to watch over us when mom found employment in a major department store downtown. Living in El Barrio ended in a few short years when our family was relocated to Queens Bridge Housing in Long Island City, a large, public housing complex situated in an industrial area on the Queens side of the Queensboro Bridge. One authoritative source suggests the motive was to integrate a development that was largely "White." What I do know is that the move put a physical and psychological barrier between family and friends who remained in East Harlem. This forced my immediate family to interact with others who lived in an area where Spanish was not likely to be heard, either in public or private spaces. Even so, the move brought some benefits. My father was closer to Silvercup; my mother to a new job at the Eagle Electric factory. Now both were within walking distance from home. In contrast, the elementary school I attended seemed a long way from home. It was in Queens where I had my first big performance (in 3rd or 4th grade) in a Thanksgiving play. It is amazing to me that I played the part of the narrator dressed as a pilgrim. I wonder if my selection as narrator was intended to increase my practice of English or to accelerate my Americanization.

Children's television programming also provided exposure to English at home. I was a regular viewer of "Ding Dong School" with Miss Frances, a credentialed early childhood teacher. She had a sweet and gentle manner likely to make any child feel she was talking only to her. I also watched "The Howdy Doody Show," more entertaining than instructive, fast paced, and louder. Its opening lines remain vivid all these years later, "Hey kids, what time is it?" with the response: "It's Howdy Doody time . . ." The program used a lot of language play. This language play fitted well with cultural practices I eventually would come to appreciate in Puerto Rico. These programs increased exposure to a higher level of English than my peer groups or caregivers were able to provide, contributing positively to my English language development. I call attention to these details because I attribute the level of academic competency in Spanish that I have attained to a strong foundation in English, especially English vocabulary, even though I do not consider English my primary language.

FIRST STEPS TOWARD BILITERACY

Just 2 years after we moved to Queens, my parents put a down payment on a four-family brownstone on a quiet, tree-lined block in the Bronx. At the time, a move to the Bronx was equivalent to moving up to the suburbs. With the burning of the Bronx in the 1970s, however, it became a symbol for urban decay and home to one of the largest and poorest Puerto Rican communities in New York City. Our new neighborhood had mostly one- to four-family homes and few apartment buildings, and was one of the most diverse working-class neighborhoods of the city. Urban planning would soon change the character of the neighborhood. While it lasted, kids of all backgrounds—Jewish, Irish, Italian, African American/Caribbean, and Puerto Rican—played together in harmony. I was entering 5th grade when we moved to the Bronx and my sociable older brother was just starting high school.

With three rentable apartments, my parents took on the unfamiliar and intimidating role of landlords. As the responsible eldest daughter, I supervised younger siblings while mom worked and dad rested. I was also expected to dedicate myself to my studies and do well in school. Support for schoolwork came mostly from English-speaking classmates and some memorable teachers. By the 1960s the majority of teachers were Jewish. These teachers had a positive influence on me. My rebellious older brother and younger sister, and many other Puerto Ricans, had entirely different experiences. It took me a long time to understand that these were not individual successes or failures; success or failure was socially constructed. My reward for academic successes was summers in Puerto Rico, a life-altering experience at a critical juncture in my social, emotional, and intellectual development.

DISCOVERING MY BILINGUAL IDENTITY

Beginning in junior high school and continuing through my 2nd year of college, my mother sent me to Puerto Rico during summer vacations, mostly with Tia Fela, mom's youngest sister, and her family. The Rodríguez-Barbosa family lived in a one-family home in Puerto Nuevo, a middle-class development near San Juan. For 2 full months of the year, I was fully immersed in spoken and written Spanish and island culture. This experience awakened my desire to understand what it meant to be Puerto Rican. It also highlighted subtleties (and conflicts) in cultural values and practices conveyed through language. My cousin Vilma mediated my entry into this Spanish world in the same way that I mediated hers when she came to New York to live with us. Informally, I was referred to as Carmencita, a diminutive that softened a name I did not like. Formally, I used both paternal and maternal last names, including my middle name (Carmen Iris Mercado Barbosa). I also learned to write the date differently (the day/the month/the year). These are two small but symbolic differences that contrast the social worlds I navigated. I have memories of my uncle's playful and humorous use of language. Although I cannot recall specifics, his use of language reminds me a lot of the late Cantínflas, the Mexican actor and comic known in the United States as well as in his native Mexico, whose films remain popular to this day.

Not all experiences were pleasurable. Entering my cousin's circle of friends, I discovered that the Spanish I spoke, a mix of English and Spanish, was stigmatized. Some interpreted my "Nuyorican" Spanglish as a deliberate devaluing of our mother tongue. Even worse, they viewed it as a deliberate rejection of my Puerto Rican identity. As my cousin explained, too many Puerto Ricans returned to the island after a few years in New York professing to no longer speak or understand Spanish, which surprised and offended islanders. What I did not understand at the time is that the imposition of English was part of a history of U.S. imperialism—an imperialism that attempted to rob us of our mother tongue. With heightened sensitivity to the symbolic value of Puerto Rican Spanish in identity formation and nationhood, I resolved to develop and strengthen my use of spoken and written Spanish. I took the challenge seriously, but it was not until I began to teach several years later that I confronted the problem as a professional responsibility. As a teacher in a Spanish/English bilingual school with a strong language separation policy, I was expected to be a good model of language use for my students, and the mixing of the languages of instruction was unacceptable.

Frequent contacts with the island also exposed me to unfamiliar practices and popular cultural beliefs. Initially, what I noticed most were my grandmother's gender-based norms for appropriate public conduct. *Buenos Días, Buenas Tardes* were common courtesies accorded others in public spaces. There was also the practice of discussing characters in popular *telenovelas* as if they were friends of the family. Although I admit to mocking this practice, keeping up with my parents' favorite *telenovelas* enabled lively conversations. It also added to my vocabulary in Spanish, especially words that were pleasurable to pronounce like *anonadada,* and I especially loved hearing dad's terms of endearment (*"mi amor," "mi vida"*) the last few years of his life, terms I was certain he picked up viewing our favorite *telenovelas* the same way I had.

I also developed sensitivity to different varieties of Spanish, especially with *telenovelas* emanating from México, Colombia, or Venezuela. And so

I discovered that *chavo* was a penny in Puerto Rico and a child in Mexico, and *guagua* a child in Mexico and bus in Puerto Rico, but that I should never say, "*Coger la guagua*" to my Mexican friends. Mostly, though, living in Puerto Rico immersed me in print, which shaped and developed my reading, writing, and speaking competencies. I began to take notice of the orthography of familiar words I could not grasp from hearing the language. The lesson for me was simple: I had to read more in Spanish in order to read and write well. Visiting Tía Cecilia, mom's older sister in Toa Baja, I entertained myself reading from stacks of *Hola* and *Vanidades* (popular Spanish and Mexican magazines appealing to women) and local newspapers such as el *Nuevo Día* that I found stashed in the corner of a bedroom. Gradually, I transitioned to complex and lengthier selections as I developed my stamina. Consistent with theories of language and literacy development, my exposure to reading (and writing) in Spanish followed a path that paralleled my development as I went from being a young adolescent learner, to being a college student, to becoming the practitioner-scholar I am today. Speaking, reading, and writing in Spanish required less effort as I gained fluency, but it also changed in accordance with the roles I assumed as I moved through a developmental trajectory that is both unique and universal.

For 2 months of the year, I tried hard to fit in as an island Puerto Rican, which I grew to understand was different from being a New York Puerto Rican, or a Nuyorican. When someone referred to me as Nuyorican, it suggested that I was not authentic and that I did not belong, in the same way that I was considered different (or exotic) among New York peers who were curious about and puzzled by my identity. Slowly, as my emergent biliteracy developed, I grew comfortable with my bicultural self. This enabled me to integrate two distinct parts of a life that seemed to be in conflict, in Puerto Rico and New York. Immersion in Spanish and intense exposure to island Puerto Rican culture at a critical period in my development served to balance the influence of my English-dominant world, strengthening both parts of the person that I am by circumstances of birth and history.

Growing Consciousness

Helpful Jewish classmates oriented me to the application systems for New York City's specialized high schools, and later Queens College at CUNY. Fears that I would be distracted from my studies led my parents (mostly mom) to prefer these friends to the few Puerto Ricans I knew outside my family circle. So while as a female I received a strict upbringing, my parents did not hesitate to give permission for me to attend dinners and participate in sleepovers when invited by Jewish girlfriends. I have always joked that my mother would have been very happy had I married a Jewish doctor. I now understand that that was mom's way of supporting my academic achievements, even though she never participated in parent–teacher conferences or read stories to me at home.

But, by my second semester in college, I started hanging out with a group comprising males from wealthy Latin American families who came to study English in the School of General Studies and their American "girlfriends." This was how I met, for the first time, a college-educated Puerto Rican male, and he captivated me. Returning to the island a few months later, he left me to mend my first broken heart. Fortunately, he wrote often and introduced me to the island's history of nationalism and struggle for self-determination. He always wrote in Spanish, occasionally long missives, I was convinced he plagiarized from a major Puerto Rican writer I cannot recall. Such was my first exposure to the culture and language of the elite from Latin America.

During one campus encounter, I said something, probably in my Nuyorican Spanish, and the response from a Latin American student I considered a friend remains memorable to this day: "¡Qué prostitución del idioma!" (literally, "What a bastardization of the language!") I now know more about the stigmatization of Puerto Rican speech, but I had never directly confronted such a brazen display of privilege from another Latino. Interestingly, a few years ago I gave a talk in Puerto Rico, and a high-level bureaucrat from the Department of Education (DIP) came up to me to compliment me, expressing surprise that I did not speak like Nuyoricans, who omit final consonants or substitute l's for r's. While I was pleased that I had made some "progress," I would have preferred to provide a sociolinguistic explanation of Nuyorican Spanish to an educated Puerto Rican from DIP.

Developing Professional Competence

My emergent bilingualism opened doors for me just as the NYC Board of Education was preparing to respond to a class action suit brought on behalf of the city's Puerto Rican students. The resulting "consent decree" with the Board of Education called for instruction in Spanish as a way to contain the high drop-out rate among these students. By now, my circumstantial bilingualism was sufficiently developed so that I passed a Spanish exam enabling me to teach in a bilingual elementary school. Entering the profession with minimum education credits came with a self-imposed responsibility to develop essential Spanish competencies.

I taught, on alternate days, Spanish as well as Spanish as a second (or heritage) language to mostly New York-born Puerto Rican children in the

Bronx. I confronted the challenge other circumstantial bilinguals encounter when they enter teaching with either social competence and/or literary knowledge of Spanish. While both are important in school settings, educators also need competencies (and practices) related to what Jim Cummins refers to as cognitive academic language proficiency. My experiences in Puerto Rico contributed to the development of basic social competence in Spanish and provided a preliminary introduction to academic Spanish. I also began the process of developing literary language through informal discussion of children's books in Puerto Rico and in New York. However, I felt far less fluent (and more vulnerable) when it came to using Spanish, in both oral and written modalities, to explain abstract concepts and develop arguments in support of a particular position. Luckily, the school where I worked had large open spaces sectioned into classrooms by movable closets and tables. This open structure enabled supervisors to monitor our use of English and Spanish, and controlled the mixing that came naturally to some of us. The open structure also made it easy to observe fluent models of professional Spanish by veterans from Puerto Rico and Cuba, who had little awareness of the important role they were playing in my biliterate development. In these early years of teaching, neither students nor colleagues suspected that I compensated for uncertainties in using Spanish by rehearsing vocabulary and questions needed to teach on a weekly basis. The hard work paid off. I was offered a position in a new Title VII bilingual teacher training project directed by José Vásquez at Hunter College, and a fellowship to complete doctoral studies in bilingual education at Fordham University.

Later, as a new professor, I taught mostly in the bilingual education program with the support of Professor Vásquez, my mentor and boss. He was an island-educated Puerto Rican, and I admired and wanted to emulate his use of academic Spanish. How could I advocate for the benefits of bilingual education and bilingualism and not dare to speak and write in Spanish in the bilingual education courses I taught?

I began by building stamina for reading increasingly lengthier works in Spanish. I will never forget the sense of accomplishment when I finished *A Orillas de Río Piedra me Senté y Lloré,* a popular work of fiction by Latin America's best selling author, Paulo Coelho. It became my bridge novel, building much-needed confidence and self-esteem to transition to more challenging texts—nonfiction texts of increasing length and complexity focused on the professional content knowledge I needed in order to teach. I searched for manageable selections from major Spanish presses accessed on-line and felt I reached a milestone when I grew fluent reading articles from Spain's leading newspaper, *El País.* Gradually, I worked my way up to scholarly articles written on compelling topics that were the equivalent (not translations) of articles I read in English.

At a recent conference in Costa Rica I heard and read this insightful quote: *"El uso del idioma para entenderlo bien no se puede estudiar solamente de una perspectiva técnica."* ("To understand a language well you must understand more than its structure.") I also study and learn from environmental print, as occurred when I stayed in El Barrio de Las Letras (the literary neighborhood) in Madrid, where I found this provocative question on a wall: *"¿No se lee en este país porque no se escribe, o no se escribe porque no se lee?"* ("Do Spaniards not read because we don't publish books, or do we not publish books [in Spain] because Spaniards do not read?") The quote in Madrid helped me temper the sting of a similar quote I found long ago, in the preface to a Spanish workbook in which the author comments that Puerto Ricans do not read. Only recently have I come to terms with that persistent negative impression of Puerto Ricans, in large part by discovering the language and literacy funds of knowledge that reside in local Puerto Rican communities.

DISCOVERING FUNDS OF KNOWLEDGE

Since 1996, I have collaborated with pre- and inservice teacher candidates in the study of language and literacy funds of knowledge in Puerto Rican and other Latino households and communities using two distinct research strategies: the "funds of knowledge" approach and archival research. The funds of knowledge approach is a knowledge-building community in which families, educators, and researchers collaborate using tools and practices to locate and understand intellectual resources of local Latino households. It is a powerful way for educators to learn about indigenous sources of knowledge that exist in subjugated communities, as the work of Luis Moll and Linda Tuhiwai Smith suggests.

Studying funds of knowledge has also made visible literacy practices in English and Spanish that exist in modest-income Puerto Rican and other Latino households. For example, one caregiver we interviewed volunteered her time to assist her son's teacher in the classroom, and school administrators sought her out to do clerical work in the office because of her Spanish/English biliteracy. She was an inspiration to the educators in the research teams who were insecure about their own abilities to read and write in Spanish. While many follow the practice of writing their fieldnotes in English, I prefer to struggle writing mine in Spanish rather than risk misrepresenting families who do not communicate in English. It is a worthwhile endeavor because I recognize that my biliterate ability and the metalinguistic awareness associated with it heighten attentiveness to language and the role that each language plays in shaping understandings and relationships.

IN RETROSPECT

Looking back to where I began and where I find myself now, I know that I have grown in ways unimaginable to me 30 years ago. The Spanish language provides a bridge to communities beyond the local Spanish-speaking world I have known as a Puerto Rican educator in New York City. While connecting to Puerto Ricans on the island remains important, I now feel connected to a numerically larger community that strengthens me and nurtures my need to understand the cultural and historical being that I am. For example, I work with the Center for Puerto Rican Studies (CENTRO) to create on-line educational resources for students in post-secondary education using El CENTRO's vast archival collection. The archives, housed at Hunter College, are a repository of historical documents that chronicle the experiences as well as the intellectual and literary contributions of Puerto Ricans in New York City beginning at the turn of the 20th century. The most compelling are those of writers who are biliterate such as Jesús Colón, Pura Belpré, and Pedro Pietri, whose lives connect with my preservice teachers. Regrettably, these authors are absent from C-Span's American writers Web site, a popular resource site.

Through this experience of sharing my heritage with fellow educators, I have gained a sense of belonging and acceptance that I have sought all my life. Clearly, in the quest to become biliterate, I have accomplished far more than developing biliterate practices and competencies—I have become an American of the Americas, actualizing a vision articulated by Bolivar, Hostos, and Martí. I also found my inspiration for this vision in the writings of Muna Lee, a gifted American writer who was bilingual and biliterate, and the first wife of Governor Luis Muñoz Marín. I have nurtured and strengthened social, emotional, and intellectual ties that make me whole. These ties allow me to connect the many different social worlds and cultural milieus I navigate, and that form part of who I am. My ongoing struggle to improve my native language has also enabled me to provide students and teachers in my classes with experiences and professional knowledge needed to understand their Latino students' potential for biliteracy. I consider this important in a hemisphere where Spanish is second only to English as the language of communication and business.

Mine is a unique path to biliteracy, given the historical forces that have shaped me, but the path is open to those with clarity of purpose and the determination to try. In sharing my experiences, I hope others will imagine the possibilities that lie within their reach.

Part II

NOVELAS, REVISTAS, FOTONOVELAS, AND PRAYER BOOKS: STEPPING STONES TO BILITERACY

CHAPTER 4

Literacy as *Comida*: Learning to Read with Mexican *Novelas*

Lilia I. Bartolomé

With a Spanish-speaking role model in her mother, and an English role model in her father, Lilia Bartolomé grew up bilingual. Although a strong English reader, she found the content in school texts culturally irrelevant and insipid. In contrast, at home, she frequently observed her mother, cousin, and their friends engaged in spirited discussions about the characters in popular Mexican novelas. This had a seductive pull for young Lilia, who asked to be taught to read in Spanish. As she became a more proficient Spanish reader, Lilia's English comprehension skills improved. This chapter illustrates not only how literacy in one language can support and enhance literacy in another, but how the cultural literacy practices of Latino families can have a positive influence on their children's school literacy.

"¡Buenos Días! Mina, ¡ya llegué por mi comida!" ("Good day, Mina, I've come for my food!") I can still remember my cousin Marta Lydia's jubilant Sinaloan hollering on arrival at our house, demanding access to my mother's stash of Mexican *novelas*. She likened the books to the *comida* she needed for her survival, especially after a long week of cleaning other people's homes. At a historical moment in time, when working-poor Mexicana/os and Chicana/os had few recreational outlets, these *novelas* provided my mother and her companions entertainment and an escape from their difficult lives.

Even now, I can still feel the excitement Marta Lydia created in our little house, located at the nexus of two dirt streets in the Shelltown barrio of southeast San Diego. It was the mid-1960s, and Marta Lydia had recently come to San Diego from Sinaloa, Mexico, my mother's home state, to work as a housekeeper for a White American family. On weekends, she typically visited us. Part of the socializing ritual included trading and discussing *novelas*, also known as *historietas*, featuring comic book–style illustrations and text. My mother typically kept a large paper grocery bag filled to the brink with these books, which included *Memín Pinguín* and *Lágrimas y Risas*.

Memín Pinguín was a weekly comic book series that described the life of Memín (a nickname for Guillermo) Pinguín (slang for "rascal"), a little Black boy growing up in Mexico City, where he lived with his beloved Ma' Linda. Each week's comic brought new tales about the adventures and hijinks of Memín and his three friends. (In later years, I would come to understand that the books portrayed the Black characters in a stereotypically negative, racist manner.) As a child I adored this comic book because of its loving portrayal of friendship and family life. I especially identified with the close and devoted relationship between Memín and his mother, Ma' Linda.

Lágrimas y Risas was another serial publication, which maintained the reader's interest by ending each issue with a cliffhanger, labeling it *"continuará."* Most of the narratives were written by the renowned popular culture author, Yolanda Vargas Dulche. They contained romantic tales such as *Yesenia* and *María Isabel*. My mother also collected thicker, novel-length comic books that included a variety of genres, like *La Novela Policíaca* (crime and detective), *El Libro Semanal* (romance), and *El Libro Vaquero* (western).

This early exposure to Mexican popular literature was enormously helpful to me as I began my schooling, where I learned to read in English. Bilingual education did not exist when I was in elementary school so English-only instruction was the norm. I did not experience significant linguistic difficulties in school because I grew up proficient in both Spanish and English. At home my mother spoke Spanish to my siblings and me, and my father, who was Filipino, spoke to us in English. As a result, I grew up a balanced Spanish/English bilingual.

Although we did not have a lot of academic books at home, my mother's varied collection of *novelas* caught my eye at an early age and stimulated my interest in accessing them. After years of witnessing my mother's and her friends' excitement over each new *novela*, and *fotonovelas* (with actual pictures featuring popular TV stars), I, too, wanted a taste of this *"comida"*—especially those featuring heartthrobs of the 1960s and 1970s, like Rogelio Guerra and Valentín Trujillo.

LEARNING TO READ ENGLISH

I learned to read English with my 1st-grade teacher, Miss Pearl, at Balboa Elementary School, which served primarily Mexican and Black students. I must have been a strong visual learner, because the teacher used the "Dick and Jane" series and I did well. I was fascinated by the well-dressed little White children and their dog, Spot. It was so different from my own life! My mother wouldn't allow a dog in the house. She would say, *"¡Los animales viven afuera!"* ("Animals belong outside!") I was enthralled by Dick and Jane and their life in the large, beautiful home that they shared with equally elegant parents. Their mother, who resembled June Cleaver from *Leave It to Beaver*, was a blond woman, slim and tall, who always wore dresses and aprons that accentuated her tiny waist.

I do not remember ever wishing for a life like the one portrayed in these books, although I do recall understanding that the kind of life they represented was "desirable" and the life I led with my family in a working-poor immigrant neighborhood paled in comparison. Yet I do not recollect feeling ashamed of my parents or my family. My attraction to, and curiosity about, these very different and somewhat exotic people propelled me to want to learn more about them. To do so I put up with the strange, stilted language used in the books. I recall saying to myself, "No one really speaks that way, 'See Spot. See Spot run. See Spot and Jane run.'"

Despite the books' peculiar language, I continued raising my hand and waving it aggressively in front of the teacher's face so she would choose me to read aloud. In fact, I liked reading aloud so much that I devised a strategy for tricking the teacher into picking me. I noticed that when I raised my hand confidently, Miss Pearl would seldom select me, so I deduced that she preferred to choose students whom she believed were unprepared to read, who were distracted and lost their place in the text, and so on. Thus, I would resist raising my hand and would try to act as if

I were indifferent, shifting my body away from the teacher, looking away and pretending to be interested in some faraway object. Sometimes this strategy worked and Miss Pearl would choose me, certain that I would not perform appropriately. But I would surprise her by promptly assuming my place and reading enthusiastically, and loudly, until she was forced to stop me.

I now question Miss Pearl's punitive "gotcha" approach, which she used to embarrass students who were not engaged by her tedious approach to reading. It is clear that I was taught a sight-word/whole-word approach, and, for some strange reason, I relished it. Given the overreliance on memorization in this approach, I wonder if my early reading advantage would have faded when I encountered English words too long to memorize. This typically occurs in 3rd and 4th grades, when the famous "slump" hits many young readers because they cease "learning to read" and begin "reading to learn" by engaging with more difficult expository texts.

Fortunately, I did not experience this slump, and I attribute my continued success in reading English to having learned both to decode *and* to read for meaning in Spanish. Sadly, to this day I continue to witness the transformation Mexicana/os and Latina/os and other minority students undergo during their elementary school years. Most of these students begin kindergarten wide-eyed and excited about learning, but by the end of elementary school they become bored, anesthetized, and, ultimately, angry and resistant after years of culturally irrelevant, mind-numbing education.

Given that I arrived in 1st grade relatively proficient in English and a strong visual learner, I eventually joined the top reading group and took great pride in this fact. Coming from an immigrant home, my parents placed great value on education and made this value explicit to us. My mother often reminded my sister and me, *"Tienen que estudiar mucho para que no trabajen como burros."* ("You have to study hard so you don't end up working like beasts of burden.") Although my father worked as a bartender and was rarely at home in the late afternoons and evenings to supervise us, he would buy my sister and me large Indian Chief writing tablets. My father's instructions were that whenever we had no chores or homework, we were to sit at the kitchen table and write the numbers as far as we could. I am not quite sure why he considered copying numbers to be a useful activity, but he strongly encouraged us to do so. Like my passion for round-robin reading in the classroom, I found this rote task fun. I enjoyed competing with my little sister to see who could write and count the highest. Every now and then my father would reward us with a nickel for a job well done.

Most of my peers came from similarly loving and supportive homes, but they did not necessarily experience success in school. In hindsight, I see that my parents, perhaps unknowingly, worked together not only to prepare me for school, but also, and more important, to short-circuit any potential negative effects of my schooling. My father taught me English and helped me develop patience and a high tolerance for rote work, whereas my mother taught me to love reading and to seriously interrogate the context of a text. In the process, I developed pride and confidence, I learned to value education, and I worked aggressively to excel, even when my teachers did not necessarily cooperate.

READING FOR MEANING IN SPANISH

Curiously, even though I was a good reader in English, I did not attempt to read in Spanish on my own. I have determined that as a result of my sight-word/whole-word training in English, I was unable to transfer my word-recognition skills to reading the *novelas* on my own, despite my interest in doing so. It really wasn't until I began reading *novelas* that I began to read for meaning and to develop comprehension strategies and critical thinking skills. In fact, I am surprised at how quickly, after learning to decode in Spanish and to take full advantage of the illustrations, I plunged into actively interacting with the *novelas*.

Around the end of 1st grade or the beginning of 2nd I asked my mother to teach me to read in Spanish. She began our lessons by focusing on letter–sound correspondence. My mother used the instructional approach with which she had been taught in the elementary school of her little village of Jesús María in Sinaloa. First she taught me the vowel sounds and then the consonant sounds. I learned the letters and their corresponding sounds, and how to apply these decoding skills to words that held meaning for me, effortlessly. I also asked my mother to teach me the alphabet. After I mastered the sounds, my mother taught me to read syllables—ma, me, mi, mo, mu—and then helped me combine and recombine them into real and nonsense words.

I loved it! I saw it as a game, and being able to create meaningful words on my own made me feel so powerful. Eventually my mother asked me to read the complete sentences that are typically used in Mexican 1st-grade classrooms: *"Mi mamá me ama. Memo ama a su mamá."* ("My mother loves me. Memo loves his mother.") Sometimes the sentences reflected our life—*"Lilia es una niña estudiosa."* ("Lilia is a studious girl.")—and at other times they were playfully taunting—*"A veces, Lilia es una niña traviesa y burra. Lilia es una niña apestosa."* ("Sometimes Lilia is a mischievous and stubborn girl. Lilia is a stinky girl.") I got such a big laugh when we played with language like this. To test me, my mother also dictated letters, syllables, and words. Later she helped me write letters to my grandmother and other relatives in Mexico.

To this day, I marvel at my mother's ability to teach me to read in Spanish. I cannot help but wonder how it was possible for a woman with limited schooling to be such an effective reading teacher, when teachers in U.S. schools who have bachelor's and master's degrees seem incapable of teaching Mexicano/Latino students to read.

I believed I had a "secret" about reading that no one else had, and that I could transfer these secret decoding skills to English. I sensed that the letter–sound correspondence was not as regular in English as it was in Spanish, but I was elated to have an additional tool at my disposal to access unknown English words. Although I was not able to apply my English sight-word reading skills to Spanish, I quickly figured out how to transfer my Spanish decoding and comprehension skills to English. The Spanish decoding skills I learned under my mother's tutelage were not all that I acquired and transferred to my reading experiences at school. From my mother's *novelas*, I learned about Mexican cultural values, practices, and views of the world. Furthermore, since the *novelas*, unlike my school texts, contained relevant and interesting cultural information with which I could identify, I engaged more actively in making sense of and evaluating the content. I did this on my own while reading silently, as well as in interactions with my mother and others. As I discuss in the sections that follow, it was through reading *novelas* that I learned to read both the word *and* the world. The end result was that I felt affirmed and proud of my language and culture at a very young age, although, of course, at the time I did not have the maturity or language to express these sentiments.

As I grew more mature, I understood the political significance of maintaining my language and culture. In the 1970s, I was exposed to various liberation philosophies, such as those of the Nation of Islam and the Brown Berets. When I was 11 or 12 years old I used to take walks up the hill to the Thrifty Drug Store to buy ice cream during the summer. There, on the corner of National Avenue and 36th Street, I was held spellbound by the Nation of Islam's *Muhammad Speaks* newspaper distributor. As he lectured about Whites' subordination of Blacks and Browns, he asked me, "Little Brown sister, do you know that your Brown brothers are dying in disproportionate numbers in Vietnam?" I would gratefully accept the newspaper he offered me free of charge and add it to my cache of reading materials at home.

DEVELOPING A PROUD CULTURAL IDENTITY

At home I began to use my skills to read about romance, betrayal, and, worst of all, the loss of virginity experienced by girls who did not obey their mothers and went off with boys. I also learned a great deal about Mexican culture from reading the various types of *novelas*. I had not previously realized that there was such a thing as Mexican culture. I believe that I did not understand the concepts of nationality and culture before exploring the world of *novelas*. While I recognized that some people spoke Spanish and others spoke English, and had heard the term *gringos* used to refer to White Americans, I do not recall identifying as Mexican at such a young age. In fact, it was language, Mexican Spanish, my mother's language—and not ethnicity or nationality—with which I identified, and the *novelas* and comic books were written in my beloved language.

Through these texts I broadened my vocabulary and learned about cultural worldviews, such as gender roles. Since my family was not particularly traditional and my mother was the dominant force in our household, I was always a bit shocked to read about the subservient life circumstances of many of the female characters in the *El Libro Semanal* stories. One common theme in these stories was that the heroine was a long-suffering wife and mother who put up with her husband's psychological and sometimes physical mistreatment, and yet she lovingly forgave him when he finally expressed remorse.

Angry indignation burned my cheeks because I felt it just wasn't fair for a woman to have to forgive a man after enduring so many humiliations. More than once I approached my mother or other female relative to furiously express my anger at the *tonta* (dumb) female character, only to be told that, yes, most of the *novelas* portrayed good women as stupid and that I should learn not to confuse *"ser noble, con ser tonta"* ("being kind with being dumb"). My female relatives took the opportunity to instill in me the belief that women should be proud and dignified and bow down to no man. In fact, we celebrated the very rare story lines in which the woman fought back, left her abusive spouse, and established a more loving and egalitarian relationship with another man. Despite the sexist nature of the literature, I relished reading and discussing the various narratives, as well as challenging the dubious morals of some of the stories.

Other morals and life lessons emerged from these readings: I learned that mothers were to be unconditionally loved and respected by their children. I learned that family members were supposed to love and support one another. I learned that dutiful daughters listened to their parents (particularly their mothers), and I learned that one should always pray to the

Virgen de Guadalupe to ask for help with life's problems. Granted, the version of Mexican culture presented in the *novelas* was static, stereotypical, and not at all critical. Nevertheless, I found it gratifying (although I could not articulate it at the time) that Spanish speakers—people just like my family and me—occupied the pages of these *novelas*.

The illustrations in *El Libro Semanal* consisted of women with unrealistically voluptuous figures, but I discovered an interesting feature early on: The heroines were typically brunettes, while the villainesses were blondes. This had a tremendous impact on me because the opposite was typically the case on American television shows, such as *Bewitched,* in which the blonde witch Samantha was good and her brunette cousin Serena was evil. As a brunette myself, I greatly enjoyed the fact that in the world of *novelas*, brunettes were the morally superior human beings. Even at a young age, I grasped and rejected the notion of what constituted beauty in the dominant culture because it was counter to what I and other Mexicans looked like. I even convinced myself that brunettes were prettier than blondes, even though there really was no difference in the facial illustrations. All the characters were depicted with European features, although at times the villainesses were drawn with indigenous or "dark" features—something I did not grasp until I was older and able to discern racist undertones.

My consistent reaction after reading these *novelas* was the positive feeling of seeing that the people represented in the stories were like my family and me. *Novelas* depicted Mexicans and Spanish-speaking characters across the social strata, the poor, working class, middle and upper classes. Thus I understood early on that, unlike life in my barrio where Spanish speakers worked like *burros* (beasts of burden) at hard and dirty jobs, worlds existed where Spanish speakers wore suits and fancy dresses and worked as bosses, lawyers, teachers, and doctors. This was confirmed when I was older and visited Mexico, where I personally witnessed the existence of educated and professional Mexicans.

On a trip to Mexico when I was about 17 years old, one of my uncles asked me, "'*Mija,*' ¿*tiene novio?*" (Does my "daughter" have a boyfriend?) When I answered yes, he asked me what my boyfriend did for a living. I responded that he worked in a shipyard, an *astillero* (the majority of the boys in my neighborhood went to work in the local shipyard after high school graduation). Surprised, my uncle asked: "Why do you have a boyfriend who works in a shipyard? An educated girl like you needs to have a boyfriend who is a professional—a lawyer or a doctor." I struggled to explain to him that life in the United States for Mexicans was not like life in Mexico, and that if I wanted to marry a Mexican I would probably not be able to marry a professional, since most Mexican men in the United States did not have the opportunity to become professionals.

I will never forget the incredulous look on my uncle's face when he heard my not very sophisticated explanation. Only after personally experiencing attempts to subordinate me, and after studying my people's history of colonization in the United States, did I come to understand the historically low status of Mexicanos and Chicanos in the United States. I learned how this status is the by-product of oppression and discriminatory practices imposed by the dominant White culture.

LITERACY AS *COMIDA*

Learning to read at my mother's side, in my mother's language, and participating in the discussion and trading of *novelas* with her and her female friends and relatives indisputably constituted the pivotal reading instruction experience of my childhood. Each *novela* was a closer stepping stone to biliteracy. In fact, reading *novelas* laid the foundation for my later ability to read academic texts equally successfully in both languages. By reading *novelas*, I was given valuable opportunities to analyze, critique, and dissect a variety of narratives and genres. Together with those women, I "constructed" text to understand the author's intent, critiqued or "deconstructed" the content, and "reconstructed" the *novelas* to envision happier and more socially just endings for the underdog characters portrayed in the *novelas*. In fact, learning and applying decoding, comprehension, and critical thinking skills when reading *novelas* constituted precisely the type of literacy practice that would be required of me in later grades, and I quickly transferred my enthusiasm for reading in Spanish to English.

When the county-operated bookmobile visited my community, I stocked up on English and whatever Spanish language library books were available. Later, during my last 2 years in high school, when my family moved out of the ghetto and "up" to a lower-middle-class/working-class community, I took Spanish classes. In college I signed up for Spanish literature courses and completed a summer Spanish language program in Guadalajara, Mexico. When I took the SAT in preparation for college, I recalled the formal Spanish modeled by the upper-class *novela* characters to help me complete many of the vocabulary test items that reflected Latin roots. Latinized words that predominated in the Spanish I learned at home, and which the school viewed as worthless except in Spanish class, resurfaced as sophisticated vocabulary questions on the SAT. This pedagogical contradiction is so obvious that it requires no further comment.

I now clearly understand my parents' vital role in my reading acquisition process. Even though the reading instruction my mother used was merely a reproduction of the classroom teaching she had experienced, her willingness to take the time to teach me how to read in Spanish, and her own love for reading, transcended the limitations of the approach she used.

Throughout my childhood and adolescence, before taking formal Spanish classes in high school and college, I had opportunities to maintain my Spanish oral and literacy skills by communicating with family members in Mexico. My older cousin Jesús ("Chuy" to us) was a particularly influential person in my language and academic development. He was the first member of my family to earn a doctorate. I took great pride in having a cousin who had attended college in Mexico City and completed his doctorate in biochemistry in Brazil.

Chuy gave me ample opportunities to develop my academic Spanish literacy and critical thinking skills. When I was about 11 years old, he gave me a book (which I still own) entitled *Historia de America*. It had been published in 1968 and was used as the 5th-grade history book in Mexico. Chuy pointed out the chapter titled *"Adquisiciones a costa de México"* (Acquisitions That Disadvantaged Mexico) and had me read aloud the book's description of how the United States had forcibly taken a significant part of Mexico's territory and paid Mexico the measly sum of 15 million pesos. I was shocked to learn about the Mexican–American War, and I reacted in anger because I felt Chuy was criticizing "my country." Later I was able to objectively consider the validity of many of the points Chuy had made about the history of U.S. imperialism abroad, and about its equally frequent practices of internal colonialism.

My love of literacy and learning helped to produce a proud Mexicana/Chicana who was serious about her commitment to her community. In fact, I grew up so proud and confident that when my high school counselor attempted to dissuade me from going to college and advised me to register for a secretarial program at the local community college, I reacted in disbelief. I asked him if he was confusing me with someone else, because I was in college-preparation courses and headed for the university. Fortunately, my Mexican American history teacher helped me apply to and be accepted by the University of California, San Diego. This result also reflected a cultural negotiation—I could attend college *and* live at home, as my traditional parents expected.

After graduating from college and before pursuing graduate studies, I was a bilingual teacher in San Ysidro, California. I worked for the Committee on Chicano Rights and became a member of the Association of Mexican American Educators and the California Association of Bilingual Education. Life has taught me that solidarity must extend beyond one's particular ethnic group to various groups who share—even more than skin color—past and current experiences of subordination and oppression. I personally benefited by social and scholarship programs put into place by Lyndon B. Johnson's "War on Poverty"—opportunities no longer available to Latinos and other poor and working-class students. These economic support structures need to be revived to provide educational support for students across ethnic groups. Had it not been for the California State Scholarship program of the 1970s and the Federal Title VII doctoral scholarship program, I would not have been financially able to attend college or complete my doctoral studies—no matter how much moral support my family offered me, or how well I did in school.

Clearly, home and family environments are critical factors in every child's reading success. Teachers need to free themselves from adhering rigidly to their own methods and work to incorporate students' home experiences into their reading pedagogy. My teachers would have learned a tremendous amount if they had taken the time to tap into my "funds of knowledge." I can only speculate what it would have been like to arrive in Miss Pearl's classroom and yell out that I was ready to dig into my "comida" of varied and interesting books. Luckily for me, my family literacy practices and my eventual politicization compensated for the shortcomings of the school. It is revealing that, to this day, whenever I visit my mother, I look forward to pulling out her *novelas* from the hall closet so I can catch up on my reading and engage her in critical discussions about the latest stories.

CHAPTER 5

Prayer Books and Hymnals: Textual Stepping Stones to Biliteracy

María de la Luz Reyes

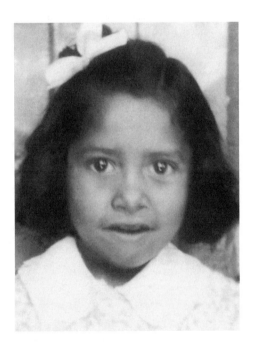

As a 6-year-old about to begin school, I possessed all the classic characteristics attributed to "at risk" children: My family was poor, my parents had little education, I spoke little English, and I had no access to books at home. To make matters worse, I was enrolling in a low-income, segregated Catholic school. This chapter illustrates how my teachers chose to overlook those obstacles, focusing, instead, on my potential and my hunger for knowledge and for a way out of the barrio. They found numerous ways to respect my culture. In reading my story, teachers (in private or public schools) may glean some lessons on how the power of cultural affirmation can yield positive results in the lives of so-called "at risk" children and how to mitigate real or imagined disadvantages.

Around age 6 I recall having a conversation with my best friend, Gloria. She asked the proverbial question posed to every child around the world: "What do you want to be when you grow up?" I was just starting school; I had no idea. My aspirations were for something better, but I didn't know *what*. In my insular community the nuns and the parish priest were the only recognizable professionals.

"I don't want to clean people's homes or wash and iron their clothes like my mother. And, I don't want to work where I get dirty like my father," I explained in Spanish. Suddenly, I remembered a man in the barrio who used to come home in a clean khaki uniform. I began describing his return home.

"When he comes through the gate, his little girls run to him, *Papi, Papi!*" my voice trailed off as if I were watching the scene unfold in slow motion. "He picks them up in his arms, then puts them down to open his black lunch box. Then . . . ," I said dramatically, "he pulls out a bag of FRITOS! I LOVVVE FRITOS!"

"He works at Frito Lay?"

"Yeah!" I said, suddenly realizing there was a better option for me. "*That's* what I want to do when I grow up—work at Frito Lay! *That* is a really *good* job! I'll come home clean and bring home *Fritos pa' todos.*"

In the Texas Panhandle where I attended elementary and high school in the 1950s and early 1960s, the major accomplishment for Chicanos in the barrio was graduating from high school. Few reached that goal. I never heard the word *college* until I was in high school, when I learned that there was a bachelor in the barrio who actually had completed college. Even then, I had no clue what "going to college" might entail. In my own family, four of my older siblings never finished high school. This was not because they lacked intelligence; some were certainly much smarter than I was, but a sense of duty to the family made them forego their dreams. Of the younger five, three of us finished high school; one went to community college and two of us completed graduate degrees. Eventually, I earned a Ph.D. In my case, I believe my birth order safeguarded me from following the same path as my older siblings. By the time I reached adolescence, our economic situation had improved enough for me to complete school.

MI FAMILIA

I was number eight of nine children born to a Mexican mother and a 7th-generation Mexican American father who had about a 4th-grade education. He was bilingual but spoke mostly Spanish at home. On few occasions, we heard him speak English with *gringos*. As a laborer for the Santa Fe Railroad, his salary was rarely sufficient for food and clothing for all of us. My teenage siblings took up whatever jobs they could to earn extra money. When it was necessary, one of us would accompany our mother to Catholic Charities where she was given a bag of rice or beans and canned goods, sometimes clothing.

Spanish was my mother's only language. Although she never attended school in Mexico, she had been provided a tutor for a few months to teach her to read and write so she was literate in Spanish. She worked cleaning White people's homes and doing laundry for the priests at the Cathedral parish. After dinner and a long, hard day, *Mamá* made time to tell us stories, riddles, and rhymes, and to teach us some songs and games. Her conversations were often peppered with *dichos* or *refranes* (sayings or refrains) to teach us important lessons, or confirm values and attitudes we should inculcate in our behavior. When one of us blamed our friends for getting in trouble, for example, *Mamá* would point out our complicity with, *"Dime con quien andas y te diré quien eres."* ("Tell me who you associate with and I will tell you who you are.") We didn't get off the hook blaming someone else. *Mamá* was also a great mimic and wonderful storyteller. In the early 1950s no one in the barrio had a television set. *Mamá's* storytelling was our primary source of home entertainment.

There were no books at home, either, except for my father's comics: *Mutt & Jeff*, *Katzenjammer Kids*, *Superman*, which he used to hide so his young brood would not sully them. I never got my hands on any of them. My consolation was that Our Lady of Guadalupe Church had plenty of Spanish/English and Latin missals, hymnals, and prayers books to go around, many with torn pages and dirty fingerprints on them.

THE MEXICAN SCHOOL

I spoke little English when I started 1st grade at Our Lady of Guadalupe (OLG)—a *de facto* segregated school in the barrio. During the entire 8 years I attended, the student enrollment was 100% Mexican American. We were all U.S. born; most of us 2nd- or 3rd-generation Americans. On my father's side I was 8th-generation American. To my knowledge, none of us had ever been to Mexico. I know I had not. We never talked about relatives in Mexico as Latino children do today. Amarillo was hundreds of miles away from the Mexican border.

Four of my siblings were enrolled in the parish school when I joined it. They were already bilingual and sporting *gringo* names: Herminia was now "Minnie," Anita, "Annie," Jesús, "Jesse," and Juan, "Johnny." I became "Mary" on my first day of school. These names became so deeply ingrained in us that we continue to use the English versions of our names among ourselves. Mary remained my official name through high school and beyond. It took nearly 40 years before I reclaimed my full legal name.

Before my first day, my brothers and sisters provided me with some helpful survival phrases in English. Minnie informed me that I should say "Please?" (as a question) if I didn't understand anything or wanted something repeated. "If you need to go to the restroom, just ask to be excused," Annie instructed. Jesse stressed that I should always say "please" and "thank you" if I wanted something, or got something. "Don't forget, you should always say, 'Yes, Sister,' or 'No, Sister,'" Johnny added.

With all those tips, I felt excited and confident on the first day. Each time Sister Mary Xavier spoke to me, I'd pop up from my seat like a jack-in-the-box and ask, "Please, Sister?" Midmorning, I raised my hand, "May I go to the be excused?" Sister asked, "Do you want *to be excused?*" "Yes, Sister," I replied and made my way to the girls' restroom. *"Parece que ésto va a ser fácil"* ("I think this is going to be easy"), I told myself. OLG School was part of a mission church for Mexican Catholics. Our "mission status" meant that our parish was an outpost of a larger, White, middle-class Catholic parish on which our survival depended. We learned to read from hand-me-down textbooks from the White Catholic school. The checkout lists inside the front covers had surnames like Kelly, Sanders, Johnson, Maguire—students who had been issued the books years before they landed in our little brown hands. We were happy to have them.

The school had four classrooms for grades 1 through 8 for approximately 140–160 students. Four Catholic nuns made up the teaching staff, with each nun in charge of two grades. Their main goal was to provide a basic education stressing "reading, writing, and 'rithmetic," with special emphasis on Catholic doctrine for the salvation of our souls. There was no library or cafeteria. We had an hour break for lunch, giving us sufficient time to walk home, eat, and return. Our playground was an empty dirt lot with four swings and a maypole with three long chains with handles where skinny little kids like me could latch on and swing around the pole.

I loved everything about school: my uniform, the books, the pencils, my tablet, and crayons. School made me feel grown up, a part of a larger enterprise where I could take an active part. My life felt organized and purposeful. Perhaps I needed the attention that was hard to get at home with so many siblings. Whatever it was, I turned out to be a good student.

OLG had basal readers similar to *Fun with Dick and Jane* except that the characters, David and Ann, had names of saints and their White middle-class family was Catholic. Children knelt by their beds to say night prayers. The primer contained simple vocabulary and one- or two-word sentences.

IN THE SHADOW OF THE CHURCH

The Catholic Church loomed large over our daily lives. It played a key role in our educational, spiritual, and social activities, especially in mine. My parents took us to Church on Sundays and on all holy days of obligation. We attended baptisms, confirmations, marriages, funerals, bingo games, and many other church functions. In those days the Mass was in Latin. The sermon and scripture readings were in Spanish for the general congregation. Special Masses for students were in English and Latin. Our parish priest was a Puerto Rican who served as pastor for more than 35 years. I met him when I was 4; he was practically part of our family—everyone's family.

Growing up around the Catholic Church exposed me to prayer books, hymnals, and scripture readings in Latin and Spanish. In Church, I found solace, solemnity, and a strong connection with other families in the parish. There was a sense of community: We knew everyone and everyone knew us. Our teachers, the Sisters of Mercy, had a talent for organizing students into choirs with two- and three-part harmony, and Church was a place where we could sing to our hearts' content. I sang in the choir throughout my elementary and high school years.

My fascination with books began with the prayer books in Our Lady of Guadalupe Church. Like other children, I quickly memorized prayers and hymns and participated actively in all rituals. I pretended to read as I followed the priest's words in Latin and their translation in Spanish. Around age 5, I first noticed that the words of the *Our Father* were almost identical in Latin and Spanish:

> *Pater noster qui es in caelis, santificetur nomen tuum . . .*
> *Padre nuestro, que estás en los cielos santificado sea tu nombre . . .*

This was a major discovery for me. From then on, I began to pay more attention to letters and their sounds. (It would be a few years before I'd learn that Spanish was Latin-based.) Soon after this revelation, I became aware that the words in the hymns, scripture readings, and prayers in Spanish also appeared in environmental print and in reading material *outside* the church. So, without realizing it, I began reading Spanish. No one was providing instruction. No one was explaining phonics or anything about the process of reading and yet it was happening in a kind of *natural and spontaneous* manner. This was my first step toward literacy.

In 1st grade, I was introduced to English reading, to the English alphabet, letter sounds, vowels, and consonants. Sister Mary Xavier lavished praise for my English reading, which, initially, consisted of one-syllable words. No one was aware, however, that I could read polysyllabic words and complex sentences in Spanish prayer books. Admittedly, Spanish has a consistent letter–sound correspondence that makes decoding easier than in English. However, I wasn't merely "barking words"; I could comprehend what I was reading beyond a literal level. Of course, the priest's homilies helped reinforce my understanding of the texts. My mother was the only one who noticed my emerging Spanish literacy. Sometimes, she'd ask me to read her brother's letters from Mexico, but she didn't make a big fuss over it. She simply accepted it as a given. I would eventually become her English and Spanish scribe. Many of my peers also learned to read Spanish sometime in elementary school, although none of us received instruction in it.

UNSPOKEN LANGUAGE POLICIES

OLG School held to a policy that allowed the nuns to hold back any student who failed to learn sufficient English. The first year was called "primer" or "1st grade," depending on whether the student learned to read and learned enough English to move on to 2nd grade. This was a statewide educational policy instituted to give Mexican children a year to learn English. This wasn't explained to parents unless it pertained to their child. Fortunately for me, I learned to read quickly and was promoted to 2nd grade at the end of my first year. English was the medium of instruction at OLG. While nothing in the curriculum was taught in Spanish, the importance of our native language in our lives was clearly communicated to us. The nuns, for example, had command of a few key phrases in Spanish to keep us in line: *"Cierren la boca"* ("Close your mouth"), *"En linea, por favor"* ("Get in line, please"), *muy bien*, a favorite, and *"¡Ándale, ándale!"* ("Hurry, hurry!") Additionally, extracurricular activities such as school plays and programs were bilingual; some activities were entirely in Spanish. For September 16th (Mexican Independence Day) the nuns and our Puerto Rican pastor taught us to sing the Mexican national anthem for a country none of us had ever visited. We performed folkdances taught by some of the mothers, and memorized Spanish speeches and poems to participate in community-wide celebrations. The Sisters of Mercy integrated Spanish and English in our school performances so our parents and grandparents could easily enjoy them. Yet, except for one nun assigned to OLG when I was in 5th grade, none of the nuns were bilingual.

I was vaguely aware, via friends, that Spanish was banned in other schools and that students were punished for speaking Spanish. At OLG most of the nuns turned a blind eye—even the one they had in the back of their heads. Of course, all this respect for our native language may have been a ruse to win our souls.

ENTERTAINMENT *EN ESPAÑOL*

Bilingualism was vibrant in our parish and in the barrio. It became even more so when the parish finally built a new church and moved the old one to another side of the parish property. The old church building later reopened as a movie theater where, for a quarter, we could watch Mexican films on Sunday afternoons. *El Show del Padre* (The Priest's Cinema), as we called it, was a great source of entertainment and language learning. Through film, we soon became acquainted with famous Mexican movie stars and with the music of the era—music I still enjoy. Hollywood movie stars we knew less well, but we were up to speed in the music of the day—pop music, rock 'n' roll, Elvis, and country western singers like Patsy Cline and Hank Williams. At night, sometimes we'd listen to *The Amos 'n' Andy Show* on the radio. In this regard, we were truly bicultural.

As we moved up the grades, my siblings and I gradually shifted to English among ourselves and with our peers in school. We also engaged in a great deal of code-switching at home and on the school grounds. Mixing Spanish and English was often a way of injecting humor in our conversations, like, *"There goes the Lone Ranger y el tonto."* In grade school this was infinitely funnier than saying, "There goes the Lone Ranger and Tonto"; our complicity in the derision of Native Americans eluded us at the time. Without realizing it, the prejudices and stereotypical views of non-Whites that were part and parcel of our assimilation into the dominant culture were creeping into our psyches. At times, we were even the brunt of our own jokes.

HIGH SCHOOL CULTURE SHOCK

For the many years of washing the priests' laundry, my mother earned a tuition waiver for me to attend the girls' Catholic high school. St. Mary's Academy was a predominantly White school across town. Five or six Chicanas transferred from OLG. We called ourselves *moscas en leche* (flies in milk). Overnight, our skin seemed to turn into neon.

At OLG, I had always been at the top of my class (albeit a very small class) and was often the first to answer questions, but my first year at St. Mary's was a jarring experience. During that entire year, I felt too insecure to raise my hand except in Spanish class.

My self-consciousness about English emerged in the last semester of 8th grade at OLG when Sister Lucia, with all good intentions, decided that some students needed to learn to distinguish the difference between the /sh/ and /ch/ sounds, which change the meaning in English but are interchangeable sounds in Spanish. Whether you say *muchacho* or *mush-asho*—everyone knows you mean "boy." We never learned who had the problem, but in the end, we *all* acquired it. There were 15-minute drills *every* day that semester. On our return from lunch, we'd find the front board covered with columns of words containing /sh/ and /ch/. After a quick review of the words, Sister Lucia would point to a word and call a student's name at random. Our affective filters would rise to such a level of anxiety that we were unable to hear the distinction in the sounds. An incorrect pronunciation triggered a loud "NO!" and someone else would be put on the spot. She moved quickly from student to student. We hated these drills. I began to theorize that words with /sh/ had a softer pronunciation and words with /ch/ were louder. My hypothesis didn't pan out. By the end of 8th grade I was as paranoid as everyone else. Did I eat a bag of "ships" last night? Did I "wich" upon a star? Back then teachers did not understand how stress and anxiety negatively affect learning.

My reticence to speak up in class was exacerbated at my 8th-grade graduation, the night I delivered the valedictorian's speech at OLG. The bishop attended our commencement. After the ceremony, he congratulated me with: "That was a great speech. Too bad you don't know the difference between /sh/ and /ch/." A lump rose in my throat.

EXPOSURE TO FORMAL SPANISH

My first formal instruction in Spanish came in my freshman year of high school. Our White peers *expected* the "Mexican girls" to get As in Spanish because it was our native language. We hoped it would be so. Unfortunately, our grades depended on our mastery of grammar, spelling, and use of standard forms—and this was our first exposure to standard Spanish. We discovered quickly that a good portion of our Spanish was a substandard variety. We took it all in stride.

Learning to conjugate verbs proved a challenge, but also perfect fodder for our after-school entertainment. Going home we'd sit in the back of the city bus, where someone would call out a verb (an infinitive). Sometimes the verbs were Spanglish—words like *watchar* (to watch) or *lonchar* (to lunch); frequently it was a verb referring to a bodily function. (Ah, yes, Catholic girls could be as crass as teenage boys!) Another girl would specify a tense. The drill would begin in loud chorus, *cagar* (to defecate): *yo cago, tu cagas,* and so on. When we'd come to the second person plural—a form not used in U.S. Spanish, we'd pause dramatically and chant, even louder: "*VOSOTROS CAGAIS!*" to which would follow a cascade of laughter. We would spend our bus ride home ridiculing and practicing verb tenses in present, past, preterit, past perfect, pluperfect, and in the subjunctive mood. Time spent ridiculing verb conjugations actually turned out to help our mastery of verb tenses. In a predominantly White school, our bilingualism turned out to be a source of fun, a means of solidarity—and, sometimes, even our secret code. As we recognized this advantage, we said to ourselves: "*Pobrecitas* (poor things), they can only speak English."

COLLEGE BY DEFAULT

I made the honor roll starting in my sophomore year, after gaining the courage to raise my hand. But, as my confidence returned, I discovered that being at "the top of a class" was relative—and I was just an average student after all. This fact never deterred my efforts. Inside my head I could still hear my elementary teachers saying: "You're a bright girl, Mary Reyes!"

After high school, my girlfriends were engaged or looking for husbands. That was the social norm in my barrio. Perhaps I was a cultural mutant, but marriage after high school was not for me. I was still in search of a "clean" job. Although I didn't know it at the time, I understand now that the cultural norms in my barrio were bounded by economic practices that developed within the constraints of our unequal power relations and the limitations placed upon minorities' upward mobility. To be sure, there was a lower ceiling for all women during the 1950s, but options for Chicana/os were even more restricted by the racist and discriminatory policies of the day. At least, that was my experience in Texas.

Within a few weeks of graduation, I was hired as a clerk-typist at the Catholic Chancery where there was a new Bishop at the helm. Running in church circles made it difficult to escape the Church's influence on me, but I felt lucky to have a "good" job. About a year later the Sisters invited a group of Catholic girls to join them on a trip to St. Louis to witness the "veiling" of postulants. This was my first trip outside of Texas. The nuns, no doubt, had had their eye on me and the invitation had nothing to do with luck; it was a *recruiting* trip. About 6 months after the trip, I informed my angry boyfriend that I was joining the convent.

To my surprise and good fortune, I learned that the Sisters of Mercy required its members to select a service career and complete a bachelor's degree. Teaching, nursing, and social work were our options. I chose a double major of elementary education and Spanish. The latter offered me my introduction to great Spanish writers: Cervantes, Mistral, Unamuno, Machado, Lorca, and many others, who opened up another new world for me. I was finally becoming educated.

After completing my degree, I taught language arts in a small Catholic school in a rural German community in West Texas. Among other things, I discovered my veil was no shield against ingrained prejudice toward "Meskins." After 3 years, I transferred to a Catholic high school in Missouri where I had my first opportunity to teach Spanish. The more I taught Spanish, the better I learned it. One major downside was that I still had few opportunities to speak Spanish with people who could actually carry on a conversation. I loved teaching at both the elementary and high school level. In the early 1970s, high school students were still manageable and even malleable at that mostly White and Black inner-city school. There, my Brown skin was a welcome sight to African American students who felt some kinship with me. I was often greeted with, "Hey, Sista', are you one of us?"

After 3 years, I moved back to Texas, where I became director of three child development centers for migrant children. This was the first assignment where I came in contact with 3- and 4-year-old, Mexican-origin children who were much like I had been as a child. They came to the center with bright eyes and eager smiles, ready to soak in whatever learning activity we placed before them. Bilingual legislation had passed at the national level so we had free rein to experiment with a makeshift bilingual curriculum that the teachers and I were putting together. Those children were fortunate to be introduced to learning in their own native language while also being exposed to English through children's songs and books accompanied by movements and gestures.

All these stepping stones improved my biliteracy and my teaching skills; in effect, they expanded my horizon. The scales in my eyes began to fall as I encountered the real world with all its ugly warts: racism, discrimination, greed, inequity, and injustice. My constant scrutiny of the very same Church that had cradled and nurtured me eventually led to my departure.

LOOKING BACK

Nothing in my environment or upbringing could have predicted I would one day attend college, much less earn a Ph.D. and become a scholar dedicated to advocating for bilingual education. From an early age, Spanish was an important part of my life; later bilingualism and biliteracy became defining aspects of my identity as a Chicana and as an educated professional. Becoming bilingual and biliterate without formal instruction began as a result of my own experimentation and curiosity with the only printed texts available to me as a young child, and as a result of the steps I took on my own initiative at various points in my life. My success in moving through the educational pipeline with my cultural identity intact was due, in large part, to the Catholic Church in whose shadow I grew up, and to my teachers in elementary school who did not view my limited English, or my poverty, as obstacles to learning. Unlike many teachers today, who lack confidence in teaching linguistically diverse students because they do not speak their students' native languages, my teachers never used their lack of fluency in Spanish as an excuse for not trying their best to lift us up rather than put us down. In my case, they challenged me to reach for high academic goals by providing me with discipline and rigor, and by respecting and treating my native language and cultural heritage as valuable resources for engaging me and my peers in extracurricular activities while, at the same time, keeping our parents connected to school. Non-bilingual teachers in private or public schools can emulate these strategies; they are, after all, strategies for tapping into funds of knowledge that support students' learning. In an era when all outside forces were determined to suppress our native language, I celebrated Spanish in the safe haven of the small world where I grew up.

CHAPTER 6

Border Literacies:
Con-Textos Bilingües

María V. Balderrama

Growing up in a border town in California at a time when border crossing was a safe and common occurrence for Americans and Mexicans, María Balderrama made little distinction between English and Spanish. But she soon learned the power differential in the two languages. Her bilingualism emerged as a result of who she was and of the environment where she lived. The display of texts on newsstands on the Mexican side of the border provided inexpensive materials that she used as additional stepping stones for her Spanish literacy. In 1st grade she learned to read English from post-civil rights teachers who demonstrated cultural sensitivity. This chapter illustrates the strong language ties that Latinos have with the Spanish language and provides examples of how caring teachers can make appropriate pedagogical accommodations for them. Sadly, it also reveals an entrenched xenophobia that is hard to stamp out.

The universe is made up of stories, not of atoms.

—Muriel Rukeyser

My language and my most cherished memories have always been *juntos*, inextricably bound. Language has been the underwriter of memorable, sometimes painful lessons, rites of passage, paradigm shifts, and gained wisdom. Language seldom stands alone; it is inseparably tied to identity and individuality. I attribute my experiences to "languages"—more specifically, to growing up bilingual, a Mexican-origin female living in the borderlands of the southwestern United States. At the core of my private universe, I am bilingual and biliterate, and in this chapter I recount stories about how these *"cositas de lenguas"* ("language matters") define and voice my worldview, and how my two tongues have served as armor against domination in its many forms.

As much as I play back my mental records of growing up with two *lenguas* (tongues, languages), I cannot pinpoint the specific time or period in my life when I "became bilingual." It was like learning to read: Poooofff! It was spontaneous linguistic combustion, twice, in two languages. It was as if suddenly I woke up with an extra *lengua,* a linguistic appendage that made me bilingual. This additional *lengua* did not interfere with my life. Quite the contrary, it seemed to stretch my awareness and increase my experiences and my access to life, including becoming biliterate and learning to love the reading of the world in two languages.

BILITERACY THROUGH *CONFIDENCIAS*

My *Tía* Yaya (Idalia) taught me to read Spanish and not to fear print. She loved reading two popular *revistas*, women's magazines, *Vanidades* and *Confidencias*. I often saw her sitting on the porch absorbed, captivated by print, as if she were in another world. How can a paper with scribbles do that to a person? One day she noticed me watching her and she pulled me by her side. *"Estoy leyendo,"* she said, and asked me if I wanted to learn. *Leer,* she called this act of making and giving meaning to black scribbles. When I started school in the United States I already knew what it meant, "to read." I had been watching reading for some time, and later learned how *leer* happened during my tutorials with my aunt. She taught me the alphabet, how to sound out letters, and what happened when letters were combined, including the use of periods. I soon began to read her women's magazines, and continued to do so until mom thought that perhaps *Confidencias* had material not exactly appropriate for my age. As an emergent reader I was playing with the visual aspects of literacy, such as learning symbols, decoding, making connections, trying to find meaning in the experience my *tía* called *leer*.

Literacy in Spanish continued to develop as I had a chance to read what attracted my attention, and these were Mexican comic books. During this historical time, print was inexpensive and easily accessible for the Mexican masses. Newsstands could be found at every corner along the Mexican side of the border. Growing up in a border town had a clear impact on how I viewed, acquired, and maintained my biliteracy. Only recently have scholars begun to examine the unique contexts of border cultures and how these settings manifest power relations, including language usage. Those of us who grew up in these border towns (mine was Calexico, California, bordering Mexicali, Baja California), and who are native border crossers, learned quickly the power of language(s).

Growing up today along the Mexico/U.S. border is much different than it was in the 1960s, and these historical differences have ramifications for language usage and identity development. The international border was open, and culture and commerce moved with fluidity. Border crossers from Mexico, coming to the United States to visit relatives or purchase goods, brought with them their Spanish tongues, and U.S. residents going to visit relatives and buy Mexican goods crossed the border with great ease speaking English. Despite the politics, there was a shared economy where one of the major currencies was Spanish/English biliteracy. The border was a place where multiple codes of expression had value and border crossers were viewed as possessing treasure chests of cultural and linguistic traditions.

My family and I were active, native players in this circuitous movement of crossing political boundaries almost weekly, and our missions to Mexico involved personal matters such as getting haircuts, going to the doctor, or, for my father, buying his hats. My middle sister and I saw going to Mexicali as an adventure, as walking the border with dad meant we would get our share of *raspados* (snow cones), *coco* (chunks of coconut), and, for me, comic books. Mexicans displayed their goods, particularly reading material, very differently than people in the United States. In Mexicali I was attracted to the colorful and dramatic display of magazines and newspapers lining the sidewalks. Each newsstand was a literacy shrine designed by the owner. No two stands were alike, and they all seemed to hold thousands of magazines, each carefully clipped to a wire with wooden clothespins. As a 6-year-old I was blinded and intoxicated by the variety, size, and colors of the magazines. I imagined all the worlds one could visit if one were able to read all of those magazines, and my father indulged me by buying me copies of *Memín Pinguín* and the political comic, *Los Agachados.* These comic books were my candy, my sugar fix, my mental food, and I devoured each comic with pleasure, and later with ease as my literacy improved.

These border experiences with literacy are particularly significant in the development of my biliteracy because I grew up seeing reading as a way to access the world, and the issue of language(s) did not matter. I attribute this partially to naiveté on my part and partially to my family's support of my reading. For example, I did not have the conscious awareness that there was a distinction between reading in English and reading in Spanish, and there was no status or ranking accorded to reading one language over the other. We spoke Spanish at home, and read books in that language; in school, we spoke English and accordingly read in English. Each reality had a unique communication code, and I willingly accepted how these parallel universes co-existed, never questioning these different systems. Today, many students (as well as teachers and other adults) believe that reading English is the only reading that matters, and thus develop mental blocks and negative dispositions around reading in their first or home language. I had none of that growing up, even when English came home to stay.

English literacy arrived at our home through a set of encyclopedias, *The Book of Knowledge.* An encyclopedia salesman knocked at our door and sold my parents on the importance of books for their daughters, talking them into buying these through an installment plan. Little did we know how this 12-volume set would not only open our minds to new worlds through the new language we were learning, but also dramatically change the way we had previously read the world. *The Book of Knowledge* was hard bound with green and white covers with gold trimming on each page. The set was nestled in a special bookcase all its own. My sister and I used the encyclopedia with devotion to help us with our schoolwork. We never imagined the power and influence of those English texts (and of the language in which they were written), and how these bound papers with scribbles would drastically change our home, our lives, and our language(s). This bookshelf was a sacred repository where cultural knowledge and linguistic resources, essential for our participation in the outside, English-speaking world, were contained. These books were revered and we were to have clean hands when using them and were not to put the books on the floor. This respect for the written word remains with me today. Recently, I shrieked when one of my students was using his books as a doorstop in our classroom. I maintained these reading behaviors in my transition to English literacy, and my teachers were pleased with the reading habits that transferred from my Spanish reading activities.

LANGUAGE DIFFERENCES

The beauty of childhood innocence is the belief that the world revolves around us and that everyone speaks like us. I certainly grew up with that innocence, and when I started school there was no reason for me to believe that "others" spoke "other languages." (Even when I went to college in Massachusetts, I still believed everyone who spoke Spanish spoke as Mexicans *and* were Mexican.)

I remember my family talking about the importance of learning English, and distinctly remember a *plática* (chat) between my father and his boss that touched on these language differences awaiting me at school. I heard Mr. DuChamp (my father's *patrón*) suggest that English would come easy for me because I was young. I was busy trying to count how many times I could jump before stopping, and it was not until I grew older that I realized that they were both concerned about how I would handle the difference between the language of home and family, and that of school. I was oblivious (or did not care) about adult concerns related to language differences. When I heard my family and relatives laughing and talking in our home, I certainly did not believe that my Spanish-speaking family had any problems or hang-ups with language. I grew up believing that my family's language was rich and expressive, full of sounds and color that flavored my happy existence. I realize now that my life was a linguistic cocktail composed of an additive-ethnocentric mix of bilingualism. My family and community valued bilingualism and spoke Spanish, and so did I.

Little did I know that my father's conversation with his *patrón* was another marker in my path to biliteracy. In the 1960s, after many years of working as a *bracero* and migrant farm worker, my father took his family to the United States. My father had worked with one of the big landowners in the Imperial Valley for many years. As a reward, Mr. DuChamp sponsored his legal residency and provided a home as part of the package. Our home was in the middle of a large alfalfa field and a major irrigation ditch, an offshoot of the All American Canal, which passed nearby. Our white house was located approximately 7 miles east of Calexico, making us eligible to attend Jasper-Alamitos, the one-building country school that opened its doors to my biliteracy and language lessons. Schools are sites where language *cositas* (small matters) become language *cosotas* (big matters).

PLAYING LANGUAGE

On the playground, Jane Miller ruled. I had never heard a name like Jane Miller, and knew I could not pronounce her name. Everything about her was different—her hair, her clothes, her language *cositas*! Jasper had a large

playground covered in dirt with at least seven different play areas, including monkey bars, two merry-go-rounds, swings, and swinging rings. We
had ample freedom to move around; physical activity was a major priority
in our school. Many students in my 1st/2nd-grade combination class had
already developed friendships beginning on the first day of school, including Beatrice, my bilingual friend and cultural broker. Initially, Beatrice
had given me a lot of individual attention; but eventually the day arrived
when she wanted to reconnect with her friends, including Jane Miller.
"Vamos a jugar acá. Ellas tienen unas de las pelotas nuevas." ("Let's play here.
They have some new balls.") Beatrice was inviting me to play four square
with a group of girls and pointed out they had a new red rubber ball. I had
never played four square and was very curious about this new game, and
I followed Beatrice. I saw several girls line up; other girls were taking a
square. A blonde, blue-eyed girl was holding the precious red rubber ball;
she walked over and said something to me. Beatrice responded in English.
I did not understand what was being said, but I knew it was not good for
me. Jane Miller held the ball close to her body and with what sounded
like disdain said to me, "You can't play with us, because you don't speak
English." Beatrice translated what Jane said, although rejection generally
does not require translation. I do not remember what happened next. All I
remember is feeling hurt and sorry that I could not be Jane's friend and a
part of that group, and learn to play four square. This was one of the first
biliteracy lessons I learned and shall always remember.

By the end of the year, however, Jane, Beatrice, and I became best friends,
inseparable at school. We ate lunch together, we played together, and we
wrote letters to one another during the summer. Jane gave me her *Weekly
Readers* because she did not like to read. I welcomed her acts of friendship,
which provided additional stepping stones to my biliteracy and intellectual
growth. In time, we grew to love each other, and to this day I treasure the
memories of falling on the hard blacktop, tearing off the skin on my knees,
yet remaining focused on bouncing the ball high over Jane's head, taking
her square, and telling her in English, "You're out!" while others cheered.
These playground language markers gave me access to the social scene and
affirmed my identity as a member of the school. I went on to win the spelling bee in 1st grade only to be beaten by Carrie, a 2nd-grader, and the word
"fast." This language *cosita* did not matter to my 2nd-grade teacher, who
later recruited me for more important matters than spelling bees.

COSITAS DE COSTURA (SEWING NOTIONS)

In 2nd grade I became the official translator for my teacher, Mrs. Reba,
who called me to her desk one day and asked me if I could help her with

a language *cosita*. She went on to tell me that she was having some dresses made for her in Mexicali (in Mexico) and needed someone to help her with the translations because la *Señora* García did not speak English. Would I be willing to go with her and help her communicate? "Of course I will help you," I answered. My mother gave me permission, and the details were worked out with my family. I would stay after school, we would drive to Mexico (about 10 miles), and then Mrs. Reba would bring me home. My compensation was hanging out with my teacher (I loved Mrs. Reba) and going to the Foster's Freeze in town and getting a chocolate-dipped ice cream cone. I was in bilingual heaven.

I was not sure what to expect, but I was confident I could do it. After all, Mrs. Reba would not ask me if she thought I could not do it. La Señora García, the seamstress, smiled, hugged and greeted me in Spanish *con mucho cariño y gusto* (with great affection and joy). She would say how she thought I was really special and smart to be doing this for my teacher, *"y estás tan chica"* ("and you are so young"). I smiled sheepishly, thanked her for her kind words, and felt very special. Mrs. Reba was *gordita* (a bit heavy), and some of the work involved alterations, so there often were many questions/comments I had to translate. Do you want short sleeves? Do you want a belt? Do you want this dress to be just like the one in the picture? Let me measure the length of your arm. When can you come back? I remember standing there between two towering adults, who turned to me after each word and depended on me for their decisions. Overall, I felt very comfortable because my mom did a lot of sewing so I was quite familiar with the *costura* (sewing) culture and lingo.

What is the biggest fear for a translator? I believe it's getting stumped on a single word you do not know or cannot remember. I will never forget the day that happened to me with the word *la bastilla*. La Señora García asked me to translate, *"¿Quiere que le suba la bastilla a la falda que me trajo?"* ("Does she want me to raise the hem on the skirt she brought me?") I had never translated *la bastilla* into English. My only experience with hems had been in Spanish, not English. Suddenly unfamiliar *costura* concepts were appearing, pushing me to enter unfamiliar language territory and contexts, and I was not prepared. I was letting Mrs. Reba down! Would we still stop at the Foster's Freeze for our chocolate-dipped ice cream cones? I struggled, unable to translate *bastilla*. Desperate times call for desperate measures and I reached for the hem on my own dress. I demonstrated to Mrs. Reba what la Señora García was asking about the skirt, pointing to *la bastilla*. Mrs. Reba understood right away and asked me to tell her that there was no need to hem the skirt, that the length was fine. Who would have thought that, years later, I would use this communication skill as a legitimate pedagogical strategy with my

English learners—visuals and gestures to get a point across. As we sat in front of the Foster's Freeze eating our chocolate-dipped ice cream cones, I swung my feet on the bench and kept repeating to myself the new word learned, "Hem, hem. NO, not hen. Hem. *No es gallina, es bastilla.*" ("It's not a hen, it's a hem.")

EDUCACIÓN AND SCHOOLING

My family gave me *educación* and literacy in Spanish, while Jasper taught me to read English and schooled me in English. These are two distinct, yet integrated cultural, linguistic, social, and political dimensions shaping my identity and I believe are key elements of my biliterate backbone and ability to cross and switch linguistic codes. This was the world I learned and the world I knew. The cultural wealth I inherited through these bilingual contexts was a stepping stone to my biliteracy, and the pillar of my bicultural existence. At home we ate *tortillas de harina* (flour tortillas), *sopa de fideo* (noodle soup), and *tacos de carne deshebrada* (tacos with shredded beef); at school Mrs. Thomason, the cafeteria manager, introduced me to meatloaf, lima beans, and peanut butter and jelly sandwiches. At home we heard *música norteña* (Tex/Mex music) and José Alfredo Jimenez's Mexican blues; at Jasper we sang patriotic war songs like "From the Halls of Montezuma" and square danced. Mrs. Miller (Jane's mother) would drive up in her black Cadillac bringing cupcakes and punch for our Christmas party, while my mother, who did not drive, made *empanadas de calabaza* (pumpkin turnovers) and *champurrado* (Mexican hot chocolate with cornmeal) at our home. My mother grew herbs like *cilantro* (coriander), *yerba buena* (mint), and *manzanilla* (chamomile), which she used for cooking and as medicine, while my peers at Jasper came from families who farmed hundred of acres of alfalfa, lettuce, and carrots for large profits. While growing up I did not fully understand that I was living and learning to read two distinct worlds. Jasper's upper middle-class environment schooled me and gave me literacy and access to a hidden curriculum that extended my future academic achievement, opening doors to higher education in the country's elite colleges. My family successfully gave me my first tongue in the form of *educación*, teaching me the importance of dignified self-comportment, as well as respect for others. Jasper taught me the "other tongue" and the insider knowledge essential for school and economic success. Biliteracy takes on a different meaning, as its implications are more far reaching than speaking and reading two tongues.

POWER MATTERS IN LANGUAGE

Jane Miller's rejection of me in the playground marked the end of my innocence. In the 1970s, while I was in high school, the clarity of power matters in language became crystallized when I translated for one of my friends in our physical education class. Blanca Ramirez was learning English and we were friends. She did not understand what our teacher, Mrs. Garcia, was asking and I started translating for her until I heard a loud, "Balderrama, what do you think you're doing?" Everyone was startled. I responded weakly, "Helping Blanca because she doesn't understand you." "You are never to talk while I am talking. Minus three points for your speaking." "I was helping her," I countered. "You heard me!" Mrs. Garcia sneered at me when we spoke Spanish in the locker room, and I never saw her make an attempt to support Blanca, so I continued helping her.

My Spanish class was different. We had a feisty Venezuelan man who loved Latin American and Spanish literature and he used every minute of class to expose us to the classics and his own stories of his beloved country. Mr. Iglesias assumed all of us could read Spanish because we spoke Spanish. Many of us lacked the academic or literary vocabulary, and consequently struggled. This did not seem to stop the momentum of the class. As a way to encourage us to read, he emphasized content over grammar rules. Mr. Iglesias was very encouraging and had a passion for his subject. In fact, he was the first teacher I heard speak of colonization and who discussed the conquest of America from several perspectives. He constantly reminded us of our rich heritage and lectured us about how fortunate we were to be bilingual. Mr. Iglesias suggested I take the advanced placement Spanish test for college, validating my border biliteracy and providing an academic stepping stone.

At Wellesley College I became very interested in Spanish literature and gradually became exposed to Chicano, Mexican, and Latin American literature. As is the case in most Spanish departments, the emphasis was on Spain. In one of my classes I wanted to write a paper on Chicano literature and the professor told me that Chicano literature was not really literature. At this point in my life, I began to understand the elitism of some speakers of peninsular Spanish, and the pecking order of the literature and language varieties of the various Latin American countries. I became very conscious of language matters and quickly saw that while "all languages are created equal, some end up being more equal than others." As a Spanish speaker from California with working-class origins, my Spanish, according to many of my Wellesley professors, was clearly "less" prestigious than Castilian Spanish. My contributions, experiences, and even language (particularly pronunciation) were stigmatized in classroom discussions. Fortunately, another academic stepping stone presented itself in one of my professors, Tino Villanueva, a poet and scholar, who helped me begin to understand and articulate power matters related to language, particularly how Chicanos have been historically *deslenguados*. (The word *deslenguados* comes from *deslenguar*, used here as the act of removing one's tongue; symbolically it represents the permanent silencing of an individual. Gloria Anzaldua describes *deslenguar* as an act of linguistic terrorism because Spanish spoken by Chicana/os is considered poor, inadequate, unacceptable, and foul.) I was fortunate to find another scholarly pillar through Guadalupe Valdes, during my graduate work at Stanford. She valued my Chicana bicultural, biliterate experiences. Furthermore, she challenged me to develop my languages and unselfishly shared her vast knowledge. I now have the opportunity to extend these skills to my students and hope to be one of their textual stepping stones.

While my experiences as a bilingual tend to be generally positive, I cannot ignore the fact that biliterates today are becoming an endangered species. Schools continue to punish students by placing them in deficit and subtractive models of education that systematically ignore and erase their primary language experiences. Bilingual teachers do not fare better, as instructional programs reflect mechanistic approaches to language learning; the university setting, where teachers are supposedly free to promote diversity in all its manifestations, including language, is no different.

Other acts of linguistic racism are intertwined with sexism and are often more direct. In my own case, in 2009, an administrator reprimanded me (in writing) for speaking Spanish at the university, arguing, "It is rude to others." Other monolingual English speakers suggested that I was using Spanish to make sexual innuendos about a colleague. These hostile acts of language discrimination linked racism and sexism in a single speech act. The sad thing is that these are not isolated events, but rather xenophobic responses to the presence of Spanish in perceived "hallowed places" where those in power feel threatened by linguistically diverse and relative newcomers in the academy. They see no contradiction in working in a department that claims to be about culture and language, yet squelches the use of languages other than English. As the Latino population continues to grow, one need only turn to history to consider the possibility that hostilities will fuel a rise in linguistic racism. *Juntos* we must fight against all forms of racism, particularly linguistic racism that aims to *deslenguar* and uproot all bilinguals, including those who have fought for biliteracy all these years.

BILITERACY ON OTHERS' SHOULDERS

None of us develops biliteracy alone. I was born into a family with strong ethnic roots whose members prided themselves in their daughters having *educación* and knowing how to use their linguistic capital to communicate respectfully with others. Other family members like my two older sisters, *tías*, and *tíos* willingly shared in the responsibility of educating the children and contributed to my awareness of reading and literacy. These communal additive family models of living, loving, and learning set the stage for successful schooling characterized by loving, prepared, and skilled teachers who treated me equitably. The historical and geographical context of being "bilingual and by the border" deepened my tongues' roots and contributed to the development of a social, educational, and linguistic system that has helped me weather language storms characterized by racism, discrimination, and subordinate status.

As an academic, taking an outsider's perspective has helped me use relevant knowledge to enhance my understanding of language, culture, literacy, and power. Additionally, I have pursued questions about my lived experiences as a biliterate Chicana and scholar with native, firsthand experiences about growing up as a working-class Mexican in the Southwest speaking a language other than English. My academic writings and my talks with students emphasize the importance of biliteracy and honoring students' home languages. As I share with students in my classes that I am still bilingual after all these years only through standing on others' shoulders, I ask a simple question: What are you doing to help shoulder your students' biliteracy?

Part III

RESISTANCE, AGENCY, AND BILITERACY

CHAPTER 7

Obstinate Child

John J. Halcón

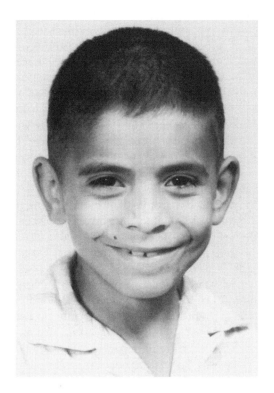

By 3rd grade John Halcón had strong cultural agency, defending his bicultural identity whenever it was threatened. His World War II veteran father had instilled in him pride in his American birthright and an obligation to master English. His mother demanded Spanish language fluency and literacy as a way of keeping her son connected to his Mexican roots. In school, however, his teachers viewed his language loyalty as a sign of "obstinacy." Bright students, like John, often present challenges for teachers who do not take time to examine the source of their students' resistance to school policies and practices. This chapter invites teachers to ponder strategies for tapping into students' emerging social consciousness in ways that foster an activism that promotes social justice and protects students' rights to their cultural heritage.

"Speak English in my house. We are American!" insisted my father. He was adamant. Our duty as his children was to learn English at all costs, including losing Spanish, if necessary. That's what he believed was required to survive and succeed in this country. I didn't know at the time, given my youthful rebelliousness, that his insistence on learning English was intended to spare us the pain and humiliation he had experienced growing up a 2nd-generation American in the pre-*Brown v. Board of Education*, pre-Civil Rights Act era. He expected my brothers, sister, and me to comply without question. I couldn't.

"NO!" My strong, independent, and very Mexican mother would counter. "*En mi casa se habla español. ¡Aúnque se crean muy gringos, deben aprender el idioma de sus abuelos!*" ("Spanish is spoken in my home. Although you may think you're *gringos*, you should learn your grandparents' language.") My mother insisted we learn Spanish to communicate with our family in Mexico. "*Español es nuestro idioma*," she would say often. "*Apréndanlo para poder comunicarse con su familía en México.*" ("Spanish is our language. Learn it so you can communicate with your family in Mexico.")

This point–counterpoint was a way of life for us, especially when we sat down for dinner. My father sat at one end of the table, my mother at the other—two points of authority vying for our minds and souls. Neither language dominated the conversation; each was accorded equal respect. Between bites of beans and rice, and *tortillas de harina* (flour tortillas), my siblings and I listened to our parents discuss topics they thought important for us to know.

My father spoke English with everyone except my mother and a handful of their friends; we dared not speak Spanish to him. My mother, ever patient but feisty, spoke only Spanish. "*Pásame el pollo*" ("Pass me the chicken"), "*Pásame una tortilla*" ("Pass me a tortilla"), or "*Te digo que te calles*" ("I'm telling you to keep quiet") were common utterances. We spoke only Spanish to her.

ANTECEDENTS

My father was born in Arizona but raised in California where he attended elementary school. He was an avid reader all his life. He left school in 6th grade to work in the fields to help support his widowed mother and younger brothers.

Segregation was the rule in public places. This was a time of "Whites only" water fountains, restaurants, and public bathrooms. Mexicans could swim in the public pool only on Fridays, hours before the city changed the water for the Saturday rush of *gringo* children. Mexicans had to sit in the balcony after *gringos* had filled the lower sections of the movie theater. These overt forms of discrimination slowly gave way to more subtle forms that would continue throughout my educational career.

Well-meaning teachers sought to "Americanize" Mexicans by changing their given names to English equivalents or near-equivalents. For some, this practice was easier than learning to pronounce Spanish names correctly. Teachers didn't hesitate to invent new ones when it suited them. Aurora, for example, was renamed "Audrey"; Ignacio became "Iggy." Some teachers even changed students' first and last names. As recently as the early 1970s, a teacher tried to call my friend Rosa Moreno, "Rose Brown." So my father, José, became "Joe." He seemed unfazed by the name change. Like most Mexican Americans of this era, he simply accepted the name change without question. When I was in grammar school I actually thought my father's legal name was "Joe."

My Mexican mother was born in San Diego, California, but raised in Mexicali where she was steeped in Mexican culture. She grew up *"orgullosa de ser Mexicana"* (proud to be Mexican), as she was fond of saying. She completed *la primaria*—the Mexican equivalent of elementary school. She never faced the kind of racism in school or society that my father did. Teachers didn't change her name, or punish her for speaking Spanish. She was proud of who she was, of her culture, language, and heritage. My father, on the other hand, would remain ambivalent and insecure about his cultural identity.

AMERICANIZATION

My father was complicit in my Americanization. He named me "John" rather than Juan. My brothers are George, Henry, and Joe, Jr., not Jorge, Enrique, or José, Jr. He chose English names to ensure that we would not be mistaken as other than who we were—Americans.

During the Chicano Movement of the early and mid-1970s when I was an activist in college, I felt pressure to change my name to Juan. Cultural nationalists, a wing of the Movement, pushed for a "return to our Mexican roots," including changing English names back to Spanish. Even though I demonstrated pride in my culture, many nationalists viewed me with suspicion because I refused to comply with the name change. I remained adamant. My father named me John; out of respect for him, that's the name I would retain.

Ironically, as a compromise to cultural nationalists, I named my son Juan, *not* John. Not too happy with me, my father insisted on calling my son John or Johnny. Interestingly, my son has never allowed anyone else to call him "John," or any other derivative. To this day, he insists others pronounce his full name correctly, pointing out that Halcón has a silent "H." Obstinacy appears to be inherent in the genes.

GROWING UP CHICANO

Like a majority of Chicanos of my generation, I came from a working-class family. When I was a child we lived in a housing project, but around the time I entered high school my parents finally purchased a home. We lived on dad's modest salary and mother's interminable patience. Unlike the stereotype of Mexican men who leave all decisions on child rearing to mothers, my father was involved in our upbringing, indirectly teaching us by example. By observing my father, I learned the value of hard work, the importance of supporting one's family, and an appreciation for education. These lessons have stayed with me throughout my adult life.

My mother was at the center of all our social activities, both at school and at home. During our elementary school years, she served as a room mother and baked cupcakes for birthdays and special occasions. She volunteered when called upon to help chaperone students on field trips. As the key figure in our socialization, she taught us cultural values and norms, respect for adults, love of country, and love of family. She exposed us to Mexican music and culture, and, of course, she bolstered our Spanish language. Our obligations to the less fortunate, and the importance of *una buena educación*, not just learning subject matter in school, were emphasized. *Una buena educación* included representing ourselves and our family in a manner beyond reproach.

ELEMENTARY SCHOOL

I grew up 30 miles north of the Mexican border in a region dominated by agriculture and cattle feed lots where there was plenty of fieldwork requiring a steady flow of permanent and cheap labor. The largely White community was the offspring of "Okie" field laborers of the 1930s who had stopped to work in the fields on their way West during the Great Depression. Many settled and established a comfortable life in the area. Returning World War II veterans, Mexican field workers, and *ilegales*, before they were classified as such, also found a small-town atmosphere and enough work to support themselves and their families.

In the 1950s, Chicanos were "Mexicans" despite the fact that many of our families had been in California since before the turn of the 20th century. *We* constituted 25% of the student body in my school. There were few Negros (as African Americans were called then) in the community, or in school. *Gringos* made no distinction between American-born citizens of Mexican heritage, immigrants, and the undocumented. To them we were all the same. We were often the target of their hostility and bigotry.

I started elementary school in 1954, barely 4 months after the Supreme Court ruled against segregation in *Brown v. Board of Education*. The indignity of overt segregation remained onerous, but would change by the fall of 1955. Punishment for speaking Spanish in California schools was common in the 1950s and into the 1960s. As much as I tried to be careful not to be too public about speaking Spanish in school, I wasn't always successful. Like others, when caught, I was punished. One teacher went so far as to record on the blackboard the number of times I spoke Spanish each day. At the end of the week, she tallied the Spanish words I had used and sent a note home to my parents, chastising them for allowing me to speak Spanish. Included with the note was an invoice charging them a penny for every word. To her credit, my mother refused to pay.

ENGLISH LITERACY

I don't recall a time when I didn't read English, or speak it. Although my father never read us children's stories, he did read the local newspaper religiously. We noticed. Without knowing it, he modeled the value of reading for us. We owned no books, but there was always something to read: local newspapers, an array of popular magazines, and my dad's perennial *Reader's Digest*— all of which were fair game if they weren't in his hands. My father introduced me to the municipal library, a depression-era adobe building that also housed the police station, city hall, and civic offices. With library card in hand, I would check out armfuls of books for my weekly reading. The municipal library was small, with a limited selection. In time, I read every book on those shelves.

My love of history comes from those early days when I first read about Abraham Lincoln, George Washington, Clara Barton, Thomas Jefferson, and others. The American Civil War held a special fascination for me. I learned about slavery, the heinous practice of buying and selling Black-skinned people as if they were cattle, that slavery was predominantly in the South, and that the blue coats and grey coats fought over retaining or ending slavery. There were the many great battles fought in places with names I had never heard of, and couldn't always pronounce: Gettysburg, Antietam, Bull Run, and Shiloh. I also discovered that reading history could be confusing. Robert E. Lee, the Confederate general, was always portrayed as an American hero alongside Ulysses S. Grant, the great Union general. That puzzled me and I questioned its logic. "Didn't Lee fight *against* the United States? Didn't that make him the enemy? Shouldn't he have been hanged for treason?" It would be well into high school before I reconciled my confusion. This explains my aversion to the sight of a Confederate flag to this day.

Reading expanded my understanding of the world and my evolving awareness of injustices against the powerless. During this time, I read mostly expository texts on a broad array of subjects: farming families in the Midwest, snowy seasons on the east coast, and snow geese in Canada that flew south each year. To my joy, I discovered that the geese I read about stopped to feed in the freshly picked fields in our local area.

From those books, I learned about the Spanish *conquistadores* and their influences on California. I studied the development of the mission system built by the Indians enslaved by the Spanish. Books taught me about the many contributions of Mexican cowboys with their *lasos, riatas, charreadas,* and American *rodeos*. Interestingly, there were not many novels, but I did read all the condensed versions of popular classics like *Tom Sawyer, Huckleberry Finn, Treasure Island,* and others. When the complete books were later assigned in the upper grades, I was already familiar with their respective plots, giving me a clear advantage in school.

The vagaries of the English language, however, could confuse even the best reader. Occasionally, I ran across a word that stumped me. When we lived in the projects everyone burned their trash in an incinerator situated in the middle of the complex, between buildings. Next to the incinerator was the proverbial government-required warning, replete with legal jargon referencing a public law. At the top of the sign was the word *NOTICE*. I thought that it was a compound word so I pronounced it that way: not ice! I interpreted that to mean that no ice was to be tossed into the incinerator when there was trash burning. It made sense to me at the time. I am embarrassed to admit that I was in 8th grade before I finally learned to pronounce that word correctly.

SPANISH LITERACY

Even before we enrolled in school, my mother dreaded the idea that my siblings and I might lose our Spanish language altogether. She understood the pervasiveness of English and the dominance of English speakers. Knowing that our American-born cousins didn't speak Spanish exacerbated her fears.

For many children, including my cousins, learning English was more important than maintaining Spanish. They spoke some Spanish at home, but never formalized it. In a personal discussion many years later, my *tia* confessed that she regretted her children didn't speak, read, or write Spanish. My mother's fears of our losing Spanish were heightened when she discovered that Spanish was banned in public schools and students were punished for speaking it. She became even more insistent that we learn to read, write, and speak Spanish well. This became her mission.

I watched my mother read Mexican *novelas* by the boxful. She also read the weekly Spanish language newspaper, and grocery store tabloids like *La Policiaca*. On her return from visiting her sister in Mexicali, she would stop at a *puestecito* (magazine stand) to purchase *novelas* for our weekly reading. In summer she purchased them by the bag full. My mother didn't much worry about their racy subject matter. Since they were the only Spanish language texts she could afford, she bought them for us.

I recall fondly summer days when the temperature would reach 120 degrees Fahrenheit and my mother would have my siblings and me sit in a semicircle on the cool, tile floor quietly reading *novelas.* This was our indoor recreation. Mother didn't provide direct instruction, but if we got stuck on a word, she was there to help. This is how I learned to read, and subsequently write, in Spanish. Reading, in both English and Spanish, were an important part of my early home life.

In 3rd grade, my teacher asked us to list all the books we had at home. When no one wrote anything, she came around to my desk and saw that I hadn't written anything either. She seemed flabbergasted, not only because I was a good student, but also because I was a passionate reader. She assumed we owned books. As she would discover, we didn't. When she asked *what* we read at home, I was able to add to the list.

Given my influences at home and school, it isn't surprising that I became bilingual and biliterate. Early on I understood that maintaining Spanish was as important as learning English. In my youthful naïveté I questioned why everyone wasn't bilingual. At the time, it was baffling to me that many of my peers didn't speak Spanish, especially those who came from Spanish-speaking homes. I was too young to fully understand the intense societal pressures they experienced and the hegemony of English.

In high school, Spanish was allowed only in Spanish classes. Even then, only a standard variety of Spanish was permitted. When my friend Omar referred to Brawley (the town where we attended high school) as *Brole*, he was chastised for his accent and use of a colloquialism. Well-intentioned teachers, much like today, thought we would learn English better and more quickly if we were prevented from using Spanish.

Teachers claimed the use of Spanish deterred us from learning English; our *gringo* peers suspected that we talked about them. We did, because we knew they didn't understand, and because we could.

LINGUISTIC STANDOFF

Early on, I learned the power of my Spanish and English bilingualism. Since I spoke English without a noticeable accent, for example, the principal made me his official interpreter in 3rd grade. I continued in this role until 5th grade, when I quit after a noisy fight and public confrontation with him. I would resume my translating after he left his position as principal, and continue until I graduated from elementary school. English was the only language allowed in school at the time so my dual language skills were often required to broker communication between the principal or teachers and Spanish-speaking parents with children who didn't speak English. As a consequence, I spent a great deal of time in elementary school in the principal's office translating for him and others.

The incident that ended my role as school translator occurred in 5th grade when a fight broke out in the boys' bathroom. We were speaking Spanish and clowning around. I said something about Mrs. White being mean to Turi, a monolingual Spanish-speaking student. Henry chimed in. Turi had been made to stand facing the corner in the back of the classroom for speaking Spanish. So when Turi tried to say something in the restroom, Eddie, mocking the teacher, told him to shut up and speak English. He was kidding, of course, but Turi was insulted and cussed him out. Eddie grabbed him by the shirt and shoved him into the washbasin. Punches were exchanged. Simple things can become serious between 5th-grade boys. The argument grew into a fight, loud enough that it could be heard outside the bathroom. Jaime left to tell the others.

By the time the principal, Mr. Thomas, arrived, Eddie had gotten the best of Turi. The punches ended, but they were still telling each other off in Spanish. Completely ignoring the fight, Mr. Thomas asked, "Haven't I told you boys not to speak Spanish in my school?"

"*Él empezó el pleito. Me empujó y le pegue,*" said Turi.

"What did he say?" asked Mr. Thomas, angrily.

"He started it," I translated. "Eddie pushed him into the sink, so Turi hit him back."

"I don't care who started the fight! I've told you boys not to speak Spanish in *my* school, especially you, Arthur. For that I'm going to punish you all for speaking Spanish."

I protested. "Punish us for fighting, not for speaking Spanish! The fight didn't start because we were speaking Spanish. Besides, that's all Turi speaks, Spanish. That's not fair." My audacity made Mr. Thomas angrier.

"You will speak English. This is America. Or you will leave. If you don't want to learn English, then, go back where you came from!" That was his typical ultimatum.

"How do you expect these boys to learn English if they don't understand what the teachers say?" I argued. Now, I was angry. "And, how are they supposed to learn English when they are always being called *dumb Mexicans* by some of their teachers?"

I was on fire. My voice cracked. Tears filled my eyes. All my frustrations spilled over. My mother's words came back to me. I had reached the end of my rope—at least to the extent a 5th-grader can reach that point. For the first time, I understood clearly that "the Mexicans" were not equal to *gringos*. I felt betrayed.

"And where do you think I should return to?" I countered, the indignity in my voice apparent to all. "I was born in California. This is my home. My parents were born here. My father is a World War II veteran. My grandparents were born here, too. Just where do you think I should go?"

"You're out of line, young man. I won't have an insolent student working for me. You will no longer be my translator."

At that point I didn't care. In fact, in my arrogance I knew he would have difficulty finding another translator as good as I was.

"You and your friends will stand along the fence in the sun until I tell you different. In fact," he went on, "I will have your parents come to see why you are being punished. I will not tolerate this impudence from any of you! I'm tired of having to remind you not to speak Spanish in *my* school. You will stand at the fence as examples for the others."

He marched us to the chain link fence, and made us stand there, facing the classrooms. The desert sun was hot. At 10:00 in the morning, it was already 90 degrees. It would get hotter. There was no shade along the fence. He walked back to the shaded walkway between classrooms and stared at us.

"I expect that you will remain standing until I relieve you. Is that understood?"

"Yes, Mr. Thomas," I said, mocking him in my thoughts. No one else said a word.

Eddie spoke up. "I'm not afraid of what he'll do. I'm more afraid of my mother. She is going to kick my butt for disobeying the teacher."

"Yeah, mine too," echoed Luis.

"We're all in trouble," I said. "None of our parents want us talking back to our teachers. It's bad manners."

The sun grew brighter. The temperature continued to rise. Students who had not known about the fight saw us when classes dismissed for lunch. They were surprised to see so many of us standing along the fence. Some came over. When we explained the reason, several joined us. Among them was Sharon, a *gringüita* friend of mine. She stood with us in solidarity. No one objected, but one of the teachers approached Sharon to ask what she was doing with us.

Angry at her response, the teacher turned and left. By now there were more than 20 students along the fence. The teachers tried to move away students who had not been involved in the incident. They refused to budge. A minute later, a contingent of teachers headed to the principal's office.

One returned with a message from the principal that any student who promised not to speak Spanish again at school was free to leave. Defiantly, I turned my back on his offer; the others followed.

Parents arrived a short time later, my mother among them, visibly angry. They were surprised to see so many of us lined up along the fence. They went into the principal's office. That afternoon my mother would learn all the details of the incident, and although she would scold me for talking back to teachers, she communicated to me that she was proud I had defended the others for speaking Spanish. My translating services would end that day.

My "obstinacy," as the principal and teachers called it, clashed with the school's "English-only" policy. I now recognize it as resistance. I found it ironic and confusing that when it was convenient for them, I was allowed to speak Spanish unfettered, but when I spoke Spanish on my own time with my friends, I was punished.

A LIFETIME OF TWO LANGUAGES

Throughout my schooling, I refused to allow myself to be categorized as either "a Spanish speaker" or "an English speaker." I spoke both; I was bilingual. I remained obstinate about retaining *all* of what I was and possessed. In spite of my insistence on linguistic freedom and success in achieving this for myself, English hegemony was the rule in schools and in the communities around me. That's how it was then and, sadly, how it is now.

My obstinacy emerged as a result of what I learned from my parents, strength of resolve and pride in my bilingualism and biculturalism. Looking back, I recognize my parents' influence on my education and my literacy development. I owe them my bicultural identity and skill in both languages. I am proud to be both American and Chicano.

When I had my own children, I insisted that they be bilingual. I became the English role model; their mother, the Spanish model. Our children would learn everything in both languages, without our imposing a strict separation of languages. They were fortunate to attend bilingual programs in elementary school. For me it was important that they also got to speak to my mother in Spanish and be reminded by my father to speak English to him. I still remember the pride on his face when my children quickly shifted the conversation from Spanish to English, then back again.

As a parent, I have been successful in ensuring the bilingualism and biliteracy of my son and daughter, but I wonder whether my grandchildren will be able to fight against the hegemony of institutions that continue to discourage them from doing the same. I trust that they will inherit from their grandfather just enough obstinacy to fight for their right to access the richness of their bilingual and bicultural heritage.

CHAPTER 8

Becoming a Bilingual Cross-Cultural Educator

Steven F. Arvizu

Growing up in the hum of his mother's cantina/restaurant, Steven Arvizu began his apprenticeship as a cross-cultural broker: serving as a scribe for his mother, translating, interpreting, running errands, trading books, volunteering to help others, and accompanying grown-ups to their medical, court, business, and other appointments. His nonconfrontational resistance and his personal agency were inspired by his mother's example in helping the less fortunate. Steven's bilingualism and biliteracy benefited from the many hours of translating, the time he spent reading in his trailita, *and his exposure to a wide genre of Mexican films. This chapter illustrates the common practice in Latino families of using children as translators. It highlights a linguistic facility that Latino children develop and one that can be tapped into by teachers as a way of enhancing Spanish and English literacy and language skills.*

As I recall, becoming a bilingual cross-cultural educator was a straight-forward journey, at once simple and complicated, at times chaotic. As an anthropologist, I know that mothers and older siblings in cultures around the world often shape language learning in young children. In my case, my mother Rachel and my sister Sarah (Sarita) played a key role in the development of my bilingualism and in shaping my moral compass. In my estimation, they were unique human beings for raising me as they did during difficult times. Besides Sarita, I had three older brothers who were also bilingual. Each of them left home at an early age. Until the time she got married, Sarah assisted in my care when I was a young child. My father passed away when I was 14 months old so I grew up in a single-parent household. My mom and I were on our own from the time I was 7 until I was about 17 years old. *Ama* never raised her hand or her voice to me. When I was a little boy, she simply allowed me to thrive in the bustle of her lively kitchen while quietly monitoring and guiding my behavior by example.

In some ways, the real story about my bilingualism and biliteracy is the role Spanish and English played in shaping my life, my cultural identity, and my career. Learning was a truly liberating experience for me so I became a teacher as a way of helping others. My commitment to working for school reform and to changing conditions outside of schools evolved over decades. I witnessed the injustices and struggles endured by *Mejicanos* and other poor people around me. Over time, I came to see the power of learning and literacy as strategic survival tools in more global cultures. Improving living conditions for the common good has always been at the center of all my endeavors. Cross-cultural competencies improved my leadership abilities as an educator and as a citizen.

LIFE ON "SHORT STREET"

"Short Street" was the nickname for Arvin Street in the small town of Arvin, California. Although only two blocks long, Short Street contained more net activity per square inch than any other part of our community. In the late 1940s, Short Street had six combination restaurants/cantinas/bars, four churches, three pool halls, two used car lots, a taxi stand, several dance halls, three markets, a movie house, the Novelty Nook, a medical and dental office, and a boarding house.

Summer was peak harvest season in the southern San Joaquin Valley—a time when the population in town would almost triple. Migrant farm workers from the Rio Grande Valley in Texas and from various places in the Southwest and Midwest arrived in droves to harvest the crops. They formed what we now call the migrant stream. Besides these newcomers, thousands of contracted *braceros* (workers from Mexico) would also come into town, but they lived mostly on the farms and ranches nearby. In addition to these, a large "Okie" population would arrive for the harvests and disperse themselves in different migrant camps. There were also a small number of American Indian and Black laborers who followed the crops. People slept on streets, on mattresses on the ground, and in their trucks and cars, reminiscent of scenes evoked in John Steinbeck's *The Grapes of Wrath*. Others squeezed into tiny rentals—wherever they could fit—for a chance to work for their mere survival. The town of Arvin was 4 miles from one camp and 5 miles from another, making us the nearest locale for shopping and recreation in the region. Short Street was a major gathering spot for many of these diverse groups and for many other entrepreneurs seeking their fortune in California, where there was plenty of work during harvest season.

I grew up in the middle of Short Street, where my mother ran a boarding house and managed a combination cantina/restaurant. On the same street nearby, two of my aunts also owned their own cantinas and restaurants. As a young boy, I hung out at two of the most popular spots around, the movie theater and the Novelty Nook. Later, as a teenager, I worked in the cantinas and roamed the pool halls. Much of my early education took place on Short Street.

MAMA RACHEL'S PLACE: MY LANGUAGE LABORATORY

Despite only 2 years of schooling, my mother taught herself to read and write. I believe her literacy emerged as a result of working in various venues and interacting with people in a community where half the population was Spanish speaking, and the other half, English speaking. Over time, she acquired sufficient competence to write notes and read letters, newspapers, and official documents, sometimes with help from her husband (when he was alive), her children, and friends. Eventually, I would become her scribe, reader, and interpreter. At her request, I learned to write her signature so I could sign official papers for her.

My mother seemed to have an endless reservoir of energy. During the course of her life, she worked in the sheds, cooked in migrant camps, ran a boarding house for *campesinos*, and also managed cantina/restaurants. Her *casa de borde* (boarding house) and kitchen were located on the backside of Short Street behind the cantinas and the theater. Everyone in the barrio knew it as "Mama Rachel's Place," and misfits were always welcome. This was both my home and my language-learning laboratory. When I was a

toddler, the sounds of Spanish and English became meaningful with rep-
etition and practice around functions of feeding, changing, napping, and
sleeping. My acquisition of language was helped by being close to someone
who made me feel safe, cared for, and loved. Growing up around my mother and sister and the many customers who stopped to eat at Mama Rachel's
Kitchen, I learned to laugh and play in both languages.

I received direction, encouragement, and nurturing from all those
around me. *"¡Qué buen hijo eres!"* ("You are so good, son!"); *"No seas chill-
ón."* ("Don't be a crybaby.") Most of the adults around me—*Mamá*, Sarah,
my *tíos, tías, primos, comadres,* and *compadres*—were primarily Spanish
speakers whose language was dotted with English words and phrases.
Nicknames became a means of getting someone's attention, or a way of
demonstrating endearment and describing character or physical traits:
Pelón (bald), *Burro, Períco* (talkative), *Esquincle* (small and wimpy). In exploring the busy world around me, I came to understand messages in both
languages and I became adept at shifting and mixing Spanish and English
as easily as those around me. My principal models, of course, were my
mother and my sister, who were comfortable in both languages.

The heart of Mama Rachel's Place was the kitchen, where friends,
borders, and strangers looking for a good meal could find daily staples
of homemade *tortillas, frijoles de la olla* (fresh pot of beans), *arroz* (rice),
papitas fritas (fried potatoes), and a *salsa picante*. Aside from being known
as one of the best cooks in our community, my mother was welcoming
and friendly. She was known to feed strangers, the homeless, and hungry
children. By observing her behavior over time, I came to understand that
food nourishes the body but the joy in preparing and serving others feeds
the soul. My mother's warm environment lifted the spirits of those who
enjoyed both her culinary gifts and her familial conversations.

Most boarders were Spanish speakers, although some occasionally
spoke Navajo, Apache, or indigenous languages from Mexico. Many were
literate consumers of *periódicos, novelas,* magazines, comic books, pocket
novels, and girlie (nude) magazines that found their way into my young
hands. As a young boy I was, at times, exposed to earthy *conversaciones en
la cocina*. Among the daily visitors were those I would characterize as *las comadres* and *los metiches* (friendly gossips and busybodies). As I helped clean
tables and wash dishes, I heard all the latest gossip, which husbands were
causing problems with their *borracheras* (drinking), which sons or daughters were stricken with *"la flojera"* or *"la huebonada"* (Mexican version of
mononucleosis or sleeping sickness). I would hear them lower their voices
and giggle over the latest *chismes* (gossip). Little did they realize that those
were cues to me to perk up my ears because something important was
coming up. My biliteracy abilities burgeoned in this living laboratory.

MY FORMAL EDUCATION

School was exciting and full of surprises. When I was age 5, my sister, Sarita, took me to register for kindergarten. When she left, I followed some kids I knew into the 1st-grade classroom instead of the kindergarten classroom. No one seemed to pay much attention so I ended up staying in 1st grade, and surviving. As a consequence of being the youngest in my class from 1st grade to high school graduation, I became a quick-study survivor—adjusting, adapting, imitating, and finding my way through mazes of new terrain—always thriving in the margins.

I was good in school and could generally figure out more difficult concepts. Because of this, my mother, my *tías*, and neighbors would volunteer my services. I was available at no cost (a thank you, a soda, or money for the movies was appreciated but not required) to those who needed help or translation of some kind. I became a pretty busy go-between for people, and the frequency of my on-call "volunteerism" increased as I became more successful in school. I enjoyed doing these favors for people, translating for them on their visits to the doctor or Kern General Hospital, and meetings with officials from government agencies such as health, welfare, police, fire, inspectors, and others. At the moment of translation, I was more focused on interacting with those around me than conscious of what language I was speaking. The difference between the two languages was not made evident until I was in school.

As a result of my frequent work as a translator, I became more proficient in English and Spanish, all the while improving my biliteracy. In the process, I gradually developed a better understanding of different social and cultural traditions and political nuances surrounding the status of people in the larger community. Crossing language and cultural boundaries became as easy as crossing the streets and moving swiftly through different neighborhoods.

When I was in 3rd grade, my mother opened our home to Josesito, a Mexican boy whose father had left him in our care. Josesito could neither speak nor write English. Being several years older than I and having some schooling in Mexico, he was literate in Spanish and helped me learn to read in Spanish. Because I was bilingual, my mother asked me to look out for Josesito in school. Of course, she only had to ask me once to do anything for her. Because of the special and continuous love she showered upon me, I would do my best not to disappoint her. *"Tu eres mi orgullo, mi 'jito"* ("You are my pride and joy, son"), she'd often say to me. So with great enthusiasm I explained to Josesito what I knew about all the various aspects of school. We planned to sit next to each other during class so I could continue explaining what was going on and what we needed to do.

Unfortunately, the teacher caught me translating instructions and lesson assignments to Josesito.

My punishment for breaking the "No Spanish rule" was to stay inside during both recesses, including lunch break, and to write 500 times, "I will not use Spanish in school." I was hurt and confused that there was something wrong when I was just trying to carry out what my mother had asked me to do. At the same time, it was humiliating to be kept inside and be shamed for speaking Spanish. My penmanship did not improve with the writing exercise, but the politics of bilingualism was imprinted in my brain and skillfully tucked away in my school survival tool kit. I *never again* got caught in that school for following my mother's wishes. Instead, I became more skillful at circumventing the rules and finding ways to carry out my mother's instructions. For most of my elementary years I went underground with my Spanish at school. Elsewhere, I continued to use Spanish for the mutual benefit of those needing the service and my own development as a person.

LESSONS IN HIGH SCHOOL

Beginning in high school and later in college, I worked to improve my proficiency in Spanish through formal study and practice. When Spanish was needed and permitted, I helped; when it was a subject of study, I excelled. Being bilingual offered a key advantage over being monolingual: I could choose when to use each language. There were benefits to each, but even more so to combining them to make important things happen.

While in school I worked my way through financial struggles by taking jobs and earning money. Beginning in elementary school I did all kinds of jobs to generate money: collecting bottles, shining shoes, running errands, cleaning yards. Later, as a teenager, I worked after school, on weekends or during summers in the fields or sheds, loading boxes onto trucks or boxcars, and with the crop dusters mixing and loading chemicals. During the academic year, I worked in the cafeteria, cleaned restrooms, swept floors, and cleaned the community swimming pool. I tried everything. I worked at gas stations: pumping gas, fixing flats, doing lubes and repairs.

Fluency in Spanish and English was indispensable for each of those jobs and led to an important transformation in my thinking when I more fully grasped the economic value of my dual language proficiency. My bilingualism opened many opportunities for threshold jobs in agriculture working with totally Spanish-speaking crews at DiGiorgio Corporation Farms. It also helped me get hired at gas stations where I could communicate with Spanish- and English-speaking customers; it helped me obtain a prized night shift job and swing shifts with the newly formed Arvin Police Department where I helped with translation. This job provided me an opportunity to continue at the local college during the day, with occasions to translate for the District Attorney's Office and for the regional courts.

SOCIOCULTURAL INFLUENCES ON MY BILITERACY

There were three other major influences on my literacy and language development. One was my good fortune to have a *trailita*, the second was *El Cine Mejicano*, and the third was the Novelty Nook. Having my own reading space in my *trailita*, an opportunity to view a wide range of Spanish language films, and engaging in social and literacy practices with customers at the Novelty Nook helped solidify my biliteracy.

La Trailita

Someone left an ancient camper on our property months or maybe years prior to my occupancy. It sat on blocks because someone, long before, had stolen the tires and rims. Sarita cleaned it up for me, putting in special blankets and pillows as well as extra locks on the door. She gave me the only keys. *La trailita* became my reading room and repository for all of the comics, leftover *novelas*, pocket novels, magazines, 36 volumes of *American Folktales*, and the complete collection of *International Folktales* from the Brothers Grimm and others. In the quiet of my own space, I spent hours reading and rereading those stories. The stories I read in that little trailer transcended time and space; they provided me hours of entertainment, enlightenment, and rich, vicarious experiences in countries and with people around the world. Years later, I studied many of these same stories in school, but by that time my mother (my first and best teacher) had already laid them at my feet.

Many years later I fully appreciate the literary treasure, the incredible gift presented to me right there in the middle of Short Street. Through books I began to see a larger, more diverse world. I learned to enter different times and spaces at will, by reading different books and stories. *La trailita* was parked on our property behind *El Cine Mejicano*. Mama Rachel let everyone know that *la trailita* was mine and if anyone messed with it, they would starve to death!

I loved spending time in *la trailita*. The morning sun warmed it and the afternoon shade and breeze cooled it. *La trailita* became my refuge from the hustle and bustle of my mother's kitchen and the commotion on Short Street. One day I was surprised by two big sets of books. I don't know if

Sarita or *mi Ama* bought them from a traveling salesperson or whether they were stolen by some *"winitos" (paisanos)* and pawned at Mama Rachel's Place, but my mother made sure I had a safe place to keep them, and I read them along with all of the rest of my books.

El Cine Mejicano

The Arvin Theater, or *El Cine Mejicano* (as we called it), was located next door to my Aunt Mary's cantina, *El Monterrey,* also on Short Street. Sarita, who had become my primary babysitter, first introduced me to Mexican movies when I was still in diapers so the theater became a familiar place. As I grew older, my mom realized it was a safe place where I could spend time and stay out of trouble. So, *el cine* functioned as my childcare facility and as a language lab, even before the schools had them. Perhaps my mother knew it might also help me with my English and Spanish as the movies immersed me in both. *El cine* became an entertaining and convenient place for me to be while she worked. Everyone knew me there as *Estevanito, el hijo* (son) *de la Mama* Rachel, and they kept an eye on me.

On Thursdays and Sundays the Arvin Theater would transform into *El Cine Mejicano,* showing movies with famous Mexican actors of the 1940s and 1950s: Cantinflas, Jorge Negrete, Pedro Infante, Tin Tan, and others. On Fridays and Saturdays, the theater would revert to the Arvin Theater for English movies. From those Spanish and English films I came to understand classic stories of the Western, Indigenous, and Mestizo worlds through epic and historical movies made in Mexico, Argentina, Spain, and other parts of the Latino, Iberian, and Arabic regions of the world. I enjoyed the magic of Mariachi music, and of *coplas* (couplets) as a dueling art form among friends using spontaneously created verses put to song *a la* Negrete and Infante to compete for the attention of their ladylove. I learned about the Mexican Muralists and of revolutions and wars fought around the world—the greatest love stories of all time, including those of personal and religious sacrifice. Historical and fictional figures like Pancho Villa, Emiliano Zapata, Benito Juarez, La Adelita, El Cid, and Don Quixote de la Mancha were not strangers to me. I came to know *La Llorona* (a fictional mother who drowned her children) who, as a child, was real to me. I had the rare opportunity to see some movies ten or more times each because of re-runs and double features.

Movies expanded my vocabulary and enhanced my knowledge of the world, literature, important events, famous artists, poets, and musicians. Some movie plots were similar to those I would later study in school. The Spanish-speaking world in all of its cinematic, graphic representations of life was there: tragedies, romances, happiness, sadness, racial and class differences, revolution, comedy, music, love, war, family struggles, and politics. Cantinflas's and Tin Tan's comedic films did wonders for my ability to understand humor and life in Spanish, especially cutting down the rich and powerful from their foolish pedestals.

Conversations and strategies for survival among the poor and unfortunate in the films, for example, were similar to *las conversaciones en la cocina de la Mamá* Rachel: make jokes about frustrating situations, have faith, continue to struggle to survive, "things will get better some day," "don't give up on your hopes and dreams," "where there is a will there is a way," or *"Dios nos abre el camino"* ("God shows us the way"). Decades later, the English-speaking world would be introduced to Mario Moreno (aka Cantinflas) through the movie, "Around the World in 80 Days." But I knew Cantinflas long before he was loved and adored by millions of people around the world. In real life, Mario Moreno—the wealthiest actor of his time (including Hollywood actors) —donated much of his yearly earnings to the poor, the homeless, and the orphaned of the world (Sibley, 2004).

The Novelty Nook

There was a hole-in-the-wall hobby shop next to my mother's cantina, one block from our boarding house and home. When I was asked or whenever I could, I would request from the vendor the latest issue of a newspaper or magazine, or I would order items in English or Spanish for myself and others. I would translate for the owner and his Spanish-speaking customers. Translating was a great way to get tips, earn free ice cream from the vendor, and gain access to the latest stuff without purchasing it.

I don't remember exactly when I began to read Spanish, but it must have been around the time I started hanging around the Novelty Nook, or when I frequented the Arvin Theater and *El Cine Mejicano*. It also could have happened around the boarding house when I began to collect books, magazines, *novelas*, and comic books. Friends and relatives did try to help me learn to read and write in Spanish. Of course, in school I was learning to read in English, and we know today that there is a transfer effect from one language to another.

Looking back, I give a great deal of credit to our year-round boarders for their help in the development of my Spanish. I would help them with English; in turn, they would help me with Spanish. Besides running errands for them, I would also lend them reading materials that I had collected from previous boarders. I also traded comic books with people in the neighborhood. In many ways, I functioned as a child librarian, dealing with pocket books, *novelas*, comic books, and sometimes, adult magazines. The more savvy Mexican *campesinos* appreciated what Mama Rachel meant to our community and, as an extension of her, I became a part of their safety net from "La Migra" (Immigration). In public places like streets, parks, and stores, the company of a young bilingual boy who knew his way around town probably offered them some comfort. A few boarders invited me to read their letters and view their pictures of family and friends. My curiosity about Mexico and Mexicans grew.

COMING INTO MY OWN

My oldest brother, Arturo, a World War II veteran, strongly encouraged me to go to college. He argued that the better paying and more satisfying jobs required more education, something I had already concluded as a high school graduate. Having experienced good teachers and bad teachers, I learned when to resist and when to pull back. After exposure to both types, I thought I could become a good teacher. Our local community college was affordable and offered a broad selection of courses with flexible scheduling so I could continue working. I paid for college by working in the fields, at gas stations, and for the Arvin Police Department.

I married my high school sweetheart, and we started a family. Most of my ideas, methods, and innovations were field tested at home with my children and later with my grandchildren.

As I worked with the police department on a midnight to 8 a.m. shift, the connections between my studies and the real world deepened my understanding of the complexities and problems within our communities. My first teaching job was with Bakersfield City Schools. The following year I became a full-time teacher under California's Casey Bill, which mandated foreign languages in the elementary schools.

Later when I moved to Davis, California, a life-altering event took place when I was a teacher at El Macero Elementary School. This school served students from the migrant camps as well as from the country club, and children of the international married students from Orchard Park at U.C. Davis. In addition, I also managed the Migrant Program in the district. As coordinator, I tried to create an infant and childcare program for migrant families to protect children from the harsh conditions in the fields. My considerable success in the classroom was overshadowed by my inability to achieve sufficient support for childcare among the farmers, churches, and educators.

That year *en los files del tomate* (in the tomato fields) a tragedy took the lives of two infants. It was a hot day when children in the fields look for shade. The two Chavez babies crawled underneath the bobtail truck to get out of the sun. Not knowing this, their grandfather moved the truck and the children were instantly crushed. This incident shook me to the core. It also shocked our small world into recognizing the dangers for migrant children in the fields. I felt somewhat responsible because I had not been able to garner sufficient support or effective advocacy to help those migrant families. Suddenly, my goal of becoming the best bilingual, cross-cultural teacher seemed like a selfish and narrow goal.

Soon after, I left the K–12 classroom and administration and sought training and educational preparation to understand and manage the change process, to engage in a more positive, geometric kind of impact on people in disenfranchised communities. My career path took a turn, but in retrospect I merely chose to work in a larger classroom setting. Remembering the role I played as a child as Mama Rachel's *"buen hijo,"* a go-between who does well and helps others, I became a leader and reformer within bilingual education, anthropology, and higher education.

Of all the teachers I had, the greatest of these was the person who ran Mama Rachel's Place—my mother. Her *cocina* was where I felt I could do anything, where I learned most about people and their dignity. My mother had the gift of being genuine in caring for others, learning about them and treating them with compassion. She encouraged me to read and to write in English and Spanish because I was needed as a "bilingual cultural broker" to help her and others around us. Her *consejos* (advice) still echo in my ears. "*¡Mijito, no quiero que vayas a manchar la bandera!*" ("Son, don't stain the flag"[i.e., don't bring shame to your culture]).

CHAPTER 9

Saving *La Nena*

Concepción M. Valadez

Concepción Valadez's form of resistance was her persistence in reaching out to her teachers as a way of demonstrating that she was a capable student, despite her poverty. The more her language and culture were rejected, the harder she tried to excel in school. Her parents feared that, like their other daughters, Concepción, too, might be "pushed out" of school. To prevent this, they made a silent vow to "save la nena." Her father spoke openly of social injustices and sought ways to right them. Despite her lack of English, her mother's Spanish note to her daughter's teacher averted Concepción's expulsion from school. The agency demonstrated by Concepción illustrates the resilience so characteristic of Latinos and immigrants who want nothing more than an opportunity to improve their lives and be respected for who they are.

Literacy has played a vital role in my family's history for more than 100 years. My parents grew up in Mexico, in an era when few people attended school, and even fewer became literate. Largely through their own initiative and some schooling, each acquired competency in reading and writing in Spanish. The Mexican Revolution of 1910 forced scores of families to seek refuge in northern Mexico, and from there many eventually entered the United States. My mother's family, which included her grandfather, her mother, herself, and a younger sister, escaped the violence and looting in Nuevo León. Traveling in a horse-drawn wagon, my great-grandfather urged his 10-year-old granddaughter (my mother) to hide under blankets in the back of the wagon as a way of protecting her from potential looters and rapists. Not long after their arrival in Allende, Coahuila, a local resident, upon learning that my mother could read and write, persuaded the family to stay there for a while. My mother was entreated to teach half a dozen children who were orphaned or left behind. So it was that my mother became a literacy teacher at a young age.

At age 16, my father was sent *al norte* by the uncle raising him, to keep him from the ensuing civil war. In time, my dad became a civic-minded man, taking great interest in the social and political affairs in the *colonia* where we lived. He followed regional and world affairs in *La Prensa*, a Spanish language newspaper from San Antonio. During World War II, a large number of Mexican American men from our community were drafted into the military to serve in the European and Pacific fronts. Because many parents of those soldiers from our town were not literate, my father became a volunteer scribe, facilitating communication between families at home and soldiers in the war zones. This involvement may explain my father's avid interest in monitoring the movement of American troops serving in World War II and his particular fascination with the Maginot Line.

UNA NENA ESTUDIOSA

Given my parents' active engagement in literacy practices, it is not surprising that literacy was to play an important role in my life and career. As soon as our fingers were nimble enough to hold a needle, my mother would teach us embroidery. This activity kept us out of the hot Texas sun and displayed our handiwork on dishtowels, as well as on pillowcases and aprons. Even as I mastered more complicated stitches and developed fine motor skills, I knew that my future was not to be in needlework.

I was around 3½ when I noticed my mother writing a letter to her sister. Tapping on my curiosity, she promptly put a pencil in my hand and told me to draw *una bolita y un ganchito* (a little ball and a hook) *esa es la letra* <a>, (that's the letter /a/) *y tres lomitas—eso dice* <m> (and three little mounds—says /m/). She explained that when you put them together they spelled *mamá*. She taught me other letters and words by describing them as familiar objects I could understand. "T" was easy to learn because it had a *techito* (a little roof over it). By using mnemonics, I discovered the magic of writing and learned that with a bit of practice I could uncover more words. Spanish words seemed to come alive magically. By merely sounding them out I could transform squiggly symbols into representations of concrete objects around me like *tomates, manteca* (lard), *fideo* (vermicelli). Soon, my mom let me write the shopping lists.

From my father I learned the wonder of reading. A carpenter by trade, my father would come home from work carrying his lunch pail and the daily newspaper. After greeting my mom, he would ask, "*¿Cómo le fue a la nena?*" ("How did the young one fare today?") Of course, there was always some calamity to report: *La nena* fainted; *la nena* fell off a bench; *la nena* had a nosebleed; she fell and skinned her shins. There was seldom an accident-free day for me. Perhaps I received special attention because I was a skinny, sickly, anemic little girl—a fact that greatly worried my parents. After helping take off my father's shoes, I would nestle in his lap, nibbling on the piece of flour tortilla he had saved for me. In the comfort of his love, I listened to him read and discuss the news in *La Prensa*. I was intrigued with the information contained in those newspapers, especially what my father shared with us.

By listening attentively, I discovered that common, everyday words had multiple meanings. For example, I learned that wars had *frentes* (foreheads/fronts). There was a Pacific front and a European front. My dad would shake his head with sorrow at the *bajas*—the loss of American lives in the battlefields. The *Línea Maginot*, I learned, was no ordinary line. Years later I would understand more fully that it was a concrete fortification with tanks and artillery along the French border with Germany. It was built to protect France from enemy attack, but, unfortunately, the Germans moved through Belgium into France from behind the line and defeated the French. The Maginot Line had an alluring interest for my father.

At one point during this time, he made a rendering of the Maginot Line on a wall in our house, complete with armored tanks and infantry. During that time, my creative and ingenious mother had a habit of painting colorful landscapes on the inside walls of our adobe home. When she tired of a scene, she would whitewash it and paint something else on the same surface. Once, while one of those whitewashes was drying, my father asked her to leave him "*un cachito de espacio*"— a little chunk of space for him to paint something. This is how that painting of the Maginot Line came about. A world event depicted on our walls brought World War II to life. My vocabulary expanded with every news item and conversation between my parents and older sisters.

In addition to my being able to read my own writing, I discovered that I could also read other people's writing. This happened when my mother schlepped my five siblings and me to Coahuila (Mexico) to care for her ailing sister. On arrival, my mom enrolled my older sisters in school. Trine, age 11, was placed in 3rd grade. Matilde, age 9, and Cruzita, age 7, went into 1st grade. My mom convinced the 1st-grade teacher to allow me to sit in class with my sisters, assuring her I would be no trouble. I didn't have to be told to be attentive. The classroom teacher was very strict. She would write sentences on the board and ask students to copy them in their notebooks. Once that was completed she would call on them to read the sentences. Most had no clue. My sisters and I observed from the back of the room where we sat. At some point, Matilde pressured me to volunteer to read the sentences. So, I raised my hand. Somewhat surprised, the teacher called on me. By that time she was already pretty disgusted with her students. When I read the first simple sentence correctly, she burst into a tirade. Instead of praising me, she shamed her class, "How can you not read something so simple that even a poor, little, 4-year-old can read perfectly?" She asked me to read the remainder of the sentences and she continued haranguing her students.

EARLY SCHOOL EXPERIENCES

I spent 1st grade in two different schools in Texas. The first school held promise because my teacher, Miss Gómez, was Mexican American. To my dismay, I soon discovered that she had her own biases; she favored *güeritas* (fair-skinned children) who came to school with neatly combed hair and clean, starched clothes. Obviously, I was not one of those *güeritas*, nor did I go to school in clean, freshly starched clothes, but I was already literate in Spanish and I was good with math problems. The two *güeritas* received treats and special treatment from the teacher while the rest went out to recess.

One time when Miss Gómez was handing back our math papers, I did not receive mine. She looked right at me, sitting in the front, and announced, "This one has no name." I had the audacity to ask, "What grade did it get?" She answered, "It got 100." Raising my hand, I muttered, "It's mine." Of course, she had known it was mine, but she asked angrily, "If you are so smart, why can't you remember to put your name on your paper?"

Despite our rocky relationship, I longed to get in Miss Gómez's good graces. One day, I asked permission to approach her desk to give her my Walnetto, a chewy walnut-flavored piece of candy (a favorite of mine) that my sister had given me. "This is for you." She thanked me and put the Walnetto on top of her desk. I expected that she would put it in her pocket or in her purse, but she did neither, so I kept my eye on her. After a short while, she walked to the wastebasket and dropped something in it. Minutes later, I asked permission to throw something in the wastebasket. I reached in and found my prized Walnetto offering.

Still intent on her liking me, a few days later I found a nickel in the schoolyard and reasoned that candy was probably too cheap a gift for a teacher. By luck, I now had a chance to soften her attitude toward me with money. "I found this, but you can have it," I said. As before, she merely thanked me and took it. When I got home that day I found out that Miss Gómez had sent word to my mom that I had stolen some money. The nickel was proof that I was a thief. Of course, my mother was dismayed that I would commit such a crime, but since my parents regarded teachers as the ultimate authority in school matters, she felt obligated to punish me. That afternoon, I got my first and only spanking. My attempts at buying a teacher's good will had backfired on me.

My sister Cruzita, who had been in 1st grade previously and was now repeating it, had not had luck with Miss Gómez either. She remembers asking Miss Gómez, "¿Cuándo me va a pasar al segundo?" ("When are you going to pass me to 2nd grade?") and Miss Gómez replying, "When you can ask me that in English!" Luckily, my family did not stay in that town very long. We moved to West Texas before the end of the school year.

A ROUGH START IN WEST TEXAS

Our move to Sanderson did not start much better for me. There, I was enrolled at Lamar Ward Elementary, a segregated school for Mexicans, where I remained from 1st grade through 6th grade. None of the children spoke English; some were as old as 9, having repeated the grade several times. Our teacher was an Anglo woman who was always yelling and making children cry. Anglo children attended another school in the western half of Sanderson, *en el pueblo americano*.

My clumsiness continued, leaving me with scraped knees and elbows that frequently got infected. When they were healing, I would distract myself by picking at the scabs, having finished the assignments quickly. My sister Trine was my English language arts tutor at home, giving me an advantage that perhaps others did not have.

One morning, when I was sitting picking my scabby knees, the girl behind me whispered something. Of course, I turned around and whispered back. Instantly, I heard my angry teacher yell, "What are you doing? You were talking! WERE YOU SPEAKING SPANISH?" I whispered, "Yes, ma'am." In a voice tinged with rage, she uttered, "How could you? You are such a smart girl!" Her reasoning was that a smart person should know better than to speak Spanish. Before I knew it, she had hung a large posterboard sign around my neck, and she was marching me in all my teary humiliation through each of the classrooms of that dusty school. The sign showed the world my sin, "I SPOKE SPANISH." That night there was bitterness in my parent's discussion. They concluded that teachers were racists. How could children learn if they were ashamed of who they were? It appeared that those teachers wanted to prove Mexican kids were dumb if they spoke Spanish—even when they were good students like me.

MY NEAR DEMISE

I developed a low profile, minded my business, and just did my work, and 1st grade finally ended. During the first week of 2nd grade, I was moved up to 3rd grade because of my good grades. School life was humming along, until one fateful day in 4th grade. In that grade, reading class always included round robin reading where each student had to endure 5 torturous minutes of oral reading. My desk was in the back of the room and I knew that Mr. Moore called students in order of their seating arrangement, so I figured I had at least 30 minutes to work on the only thing I had not yet mastered in 4th grade. (Yes, I had a pretty big head about my smarts.) I was working on a cat's cradle—a difficult string figure called "the Apache door." In Spanish, we called it *el catre* (the cot). I propped up my reading book and scrunched my skinny body down so Mr. Moore could not see what I was doing. My body language must have been the clue that I was up to something.

To my horror, Mr. Moore hollered, "Concepción, WHAT are you doing?" Sitting up straight, I admitted I was working on the Apache door. Of course, he was furious; he had warned us against playing with string in class. Taking a deep breath, he bellowed, "GET OUT! GO HOME!" Shocked, I began collecting my books as I always did at the end of the day, but Mr. Moore was not going to allow that. "NO! YOU ARE NOT TAKING ANY BOOKS! YOU ARE OUT! GET OUT!" The entire class gasped. I had never presented a discipline problem, had not ever talked back to teachers, but there I was being kicked out of school. Having no other alternative, I ran home as fast as my skinny brown legs could take me, my heart pounding, tears running down my cheeks, my sobs almost choking me. My home was only a block away. My mother immediately knew something was wrong. It was clear to her that I had not fainted in school, a frequent reason for my coming home early from school.

"*¿Qué pasó?*" ("What happened?")

"*Me corrió el maestro*" ("The teacher kicked me out of school"), I sobbed.

"*¿Por qué?*" ("Why?")

Without hesitation, I admitted I was playing with some string, learning to make *el catre*. My mother could not believe the reason for my expulsion. Quickly, she grabbed a brown paper bag, tore off a piece, took a pencil, and wrote furiously in Spanish. Folding the note in half, she ordered me to deliver it to the teacher. I ran back to school as fast as I could. The classroom door was open. I stood at the door. The teacher asked, "What is it?" I answered, "My mother sent you this." He motioned for me to give it to him. Unfolding the note, he looked at it and grunted, "SIT DOWN!" It was still reading period but he did not call on me. I sat there in a daze for the rest of the class period.

At recess my friends crowded around me. No one who was kicked out was ever allowed back in. My friends asked what my mother had written. I didn't know. They were incredulous because I could read Spanish but had not read the note. The thing was, Mr. Moore did *not* read Spanish, yet he capitulated to my mother's note. We were speechless.

To this day, I remain mystified about the contents of that note. I wonder what went through Mr. Moore's mind when he received the note. Unfortunately, I never asked my mom what she wrote and, even worse, I am not sure why I did not. What I surmise is that by the time I was in school my parents had learned a few lessons about the failure of schools in teaching their three older daughters. As was the custom of Mexican parents at the time (and to some extent even now), parents placed complete confidence in teachers and upheld their authority without question. When teachers punished students in school, the assumption was their children had misbehaved, so another spanking was meted out at home. I believe my parents had learned from the experiences of my older sisters that putting their children's education entirely in the hands of teachers, without closely monitoring their progress and the teachers' treatment of them, could end in my failure, too. Recognizing how much I loved school and how I exerted effort to excel academically, my mother decided to intervene.

Having her fourth and most studious daughter sent home must have been the last straw for my mother. She would not simply fold her hands in resignation. Not this time. No, they would not do this to *la nena*! The astounding thing, for me, is that she fought back with a written note in Spanish. Her note had the power to put me back in the classroom. Perhaps the old adage "the pen is mightier than the sword" proved true in this case. Looking back, I am eternally grateful to my mother for resisting what she clearly knew was an injustice.

"BEST GIRL" AND MORE POSITIVE EXPERIENCES

I also have positive memories of elementary school. My 5th-grade teacher, Mrs. Lindley, challenged me to excel in my schoolwork. Of course, I relished the extra attention. Once, we ran into each other in a store in the Anglo part of town where she told the storeowner (a middle-aged White man), "This is my best girl!"

"Oh . . . she cleans your house?"

"Oh, no!" Mrs. Lindley retorted. "She is my student. She's in my 5th grade—and a very smart young lady!"

Fifth grade was a very good year for me.

My 6th-grade teacher, Miss Bertha Lassiter, was a godsend. She was Spanish speaking. That was also the year I discovered a beautiful set of books in the book room (not exactly a library). *The Book of Knowledge* was a treasure trove of information that left me gasping. I would rush through my assignments so Miss Lassiter would give me permission to spend time exploring the books. I was awestruck by the descriptions of foreign countries, the houses, and people in other parts of the world, and fascinated with the variety of languages spoken in those countries. Eventually, *Mis Berta* (as we referred to her in our Hispanized English) paid our family a visit. At her encouragement, my father purchased *The World Book Encyclopedia*. And, as a bonus, we received a huge English language dictionary. I have no idea how long it took my parents to pay for that elegant, gorgeous set of books, but I rejoiced in my good fortune.

RESISTING SEGREGATION

Around that time, my father spearheaded the construction of a community hall that would be used for social functions by both the Anglo and Mexican communities. This hall, called the Club Atlético Católico (the CAC Hall), also functioned as a skating rink, another of my dad's initiatives. Although this hall was located in the barrio, it drew Anglo skaters. My sisters and I served as attendants on weekends and holidays, putting us in regular contact with English speakers. We took turns at the concession stand selling candy and gum and renting skates. Adhering to the segregation policies of the late 1940s, Anglos and Mexican Americans skated at separate times. We played different skating music for each group, big band and western music for Anglos; Mexican and Tejano music for Chicanos.

My father came up with a brilliant way to circumvent the segregation policies of that era. He instituted a personal policy that offered *free* skating for everybody on his birthday (May 11), or on the weekend closest to that date. On "integration" days (no one called it this, of course), we always had an overflow house. To ensure integration, the rule for that day was that after 1 hour, the skaters had to leave the rink for the 2nd consecutive hour and allow other skaters a turn. The result was that both Anglos and Mexican Americans would hang around to get back in the rink in the 3rd hour. I am proud to say that due to my father, we were assured that, on at least 1 day of the year, his birthday, there would be racial integration in Sanderson and free skating!

These events taught me a great deal about my parents' interest in my education and also about their political ideology. Without being confrontational, they fought against injustices and for social equality, making bold moves to break down barriers between the races. In doing so, they modeled and foretold a role I would play in my own efforts to champion the fight for equity and social justice.

I tried to apply those lessons in my own interactions with others. In this integrated 7th-grade class, I learned to use my bilingualism to mitigate tensions between Spanish- and English-speaking students. My assigned seat was between rows of Anglo and Mexican students, so the role of interpreter often fell on me. One day my Spanish-speaking classmates were talking and laughing about something. An Anglo student, TJ, asked me why the Mexicans were laughing. Having had my nose in a book, I had not been paying attention to the hilarity of my fellow bilingual classmates. I turned to tell them that TJ wanted to know why they were laughing. One smart aleck said, *"Dile que chingue a su abuela"* ("Tell him the hell with his grandmother"). I turned to TJ and said, "They're talking about grandmothers." "Grandmothers are that funny?" My *raza* peers laughed even harder. I shrugged my shoulders, as if to agree with him that the thought was silly. That episode taught me that bilingualism is really valuable, but not every insult has to be translated accurately.

MOVE TO CALIFORNIA

Two events prompted my father to move us to California. One was the fact that, although I had perfect attendance and the highest grade point average in 8th grade, I had not been allowed to deliver the valedictory speech. Racist, anti-Mexican policies in Texas schools simply did not allow Mexican Americans to hold such honors (probably for fear they might make Anglos look bad). Those policies affected students in all aspects of school life. Mexican American star football players, for example, were not allowed at the victory parties after the games. The school's solution to the 8th-grade graduation ceremony "dilemma" was that only the principal, a White male, would speak. The salutatorian, a White female student, played a piano number. There was no mention of a valedictorian. My family, and the Mexican community, were stunned, but not surprised, by the decision. Two teachers and several of my Anglo classmates *privately* offered their apologies to me for what they recognized as unfair, but there was no public outcry from anyone with authority.

The second factor was that my sister Trine informed my parents that schools in California were integrated. This knowledge, together with the frustration over the racist practices in Texas, prompted our move to California shortly after my 8th-grade graduation.

Integrated Classrooms

Our first home in California was in the labor camp in Soledad in the Salinas Valley. Gonzales High School was 8 miles away, requiring a bus ride. On my first day an Anglo girl grabbed my arm and announced that I was going to sit with her and her friends. None of those girls had a problem when they discovered I was only a freshman, instead of a senior, as they were. The high school had a fascinating diversity of students: Mexican Americans, Anglos, Portuguese-origin, Swiss Italian, and also some Filipinos. In no time, I was recruited into extracurricular activities—band, choir, sports, and the newspaper staff. By luck, I ended up in a 4th-period math class consisting of all the football players. The teacher assigned me the task of tutoring those football players in algebra. By the end of my senior year, my block sweater had four stripes and many pins, and most important of all, I had stopped fainting!

My graduation from high school brought my parents and my older sisters enormous satisfaction after the bitter racial and linguistic discrimination we had encountered in Texas schools. In California, I developed a more mature way of accepting accolades for academic achievements and was not surprised to be selected valedictorian. Although my valedictory speech had prominent pronunciation problems, going on to college was never a question.

Passport to English Fluency and Life Goals

On my own in Berkeley, I took control over my own life and studies. My early exposure to history and politics became my "passport" to greater proficiency in English. I sought friends with whom I had things in common—other "hick-town girls" who lived in my dorm. In the midst of stylish, sophisticated girls from the big cities of Los Angeles, San Francisco, and Oakland, the three of us gravitated toward one another. My special talent in reading the campus map and proficiency in using the university library system made me indispensable to my two companions. During this time I discovered that my accented English and intonation were inconsequential.

I held my own when we had lively discussions on poverty, social inequality, exploitation of resources for economic profit, and other political and social issues. Their rebuttals were models for argumentative skills and persuasive language in English that helped reinforce my oral fluency.

My bachelor's degree in mathematics and Spanish literature led to a California teaching credential. I returned to my hometown of Soledad to begin my teaching career. There, I married and had my first son. A decade later I was helping to initiate a pilot language development program in the New Haven Unified School District at the cusp of federally mandated bilingual education. My success in this area prompted me to seek a Ph.D.

For more than 30 years, UCLA has been my academic home. My association with this elite university has provided a forum for disseminating effective instructional practices for educators who teach students with backgrounds similar to my own. My work also focuses on eliminating illiteracy among adult Latino immigrants.

Strong Spanish/English skills and multicultural knowledge facilitated learning Portuguese and French, increasing the reach of my involvement in educational issues in other countries. As a Chicana academic, my presence at international forums helps to change the perception that American professionals are all White, middle-class, English-speaking monolinguals. My story is not merely a story of a Chicana, or a Mexican American, it is an American story.

POST SCRIPT

Looking back, I realize that, despite my family's economic constraints and the racial discrimination around us, I had a good childhood. Every day my home was filled with lively conversations, literacy practices, and great discussions on world affairs. My frail health turned out to be an academic advantage for me; my parents' concern for my fainting spells prompted them to engage me in one-to-one literacy activities where I could sit, read, write, or work on math problems under their watchful eye. My birth order was also an advantage for me. By the time I started school, my parents had learned not to depend on school for my education. They became proactive and must have vowed that I would not be another educational casualty in the family. My older siblings had endured miserable school experiences and yet they were my constant source of inspiration and guidance, although they themselves did not succeed beyond elementary school. Because of their efforts on my behalf, I was better prepared when I entered school. Fortunately for me, the firsthand racism and discrimination I experienced did not leave deep bitterness; instead, I learned to take charge of my own destiny, resisting social injustices and embracing my biliteracy as an important tool for my life's work.

Part IV

ISLAND AND MAINLAND INFLUENCES ON BILITERACY

CHAPTER 10

Borinquen Querido: Growing Up Bilingual in a Military Family

María E. Fránquiz

A daughter of an army man, María Fránquiz faced the challenges that come with uprooting a family, and constant new beginnings in unfamiliar locations across continents. Her literacy began in Spanish on the island of Puerto Rico but shifted to English as she attended schools on the mainland (North Carolina, Texas, California) and in Germany. The moves disrupted her schooling and required frequent adjustments to new schools, new teachers, and new students, creating undue anxiety and pain in discovering her native language was viewed disparagingly— even by other Spanish speakers. This chapter makes visible the extra challenges that immigrant and transnational students (much like the ones enrolled in U.S. classrooms) face in crossing physical and language borders. It suggests that, in addition to supporting English, teachers need to adopt strategies that help reduce students' anxiety that can interfere with learning.

"Me voy (ya me voy)
Pero un día volveré
A buscar mi querer
A soñar otra vez
En mi viejo San Juan."
—Noel Estrada

"En Mi Viejo San Juan" ("In My Old San Juan") is one of the most famous Puerto Rican *boleros*, composed in 1943 by Noel Estrada. During World War II, Noel Estrada, like my father, served in the U.S. Army with the same hope of improving his family's economic condition. Their lived experiences as U.S. soldiers resonate with the many *Boricua* men and women who feel strong nostalgia when the military transfers them away from their homeland, *Borinquen*, officially the Commonwealth of Puerto Rico. In 1971 the song *"En Mi Viejo San Juan"* was adopted as the official city anthem of the capital city of Puerto Rico, San Juan. An estimated 3.9 million Puerto Ricans, or *Boricuas*, live on the island and about 2.7 million live on the U.S. mainland—all of whom have attachment to Puerto Rico, its land, fauna, food, music, traditions, and extended family on the island, *La Isla del Encanto*.

MY LANGUAGE, MY PEOPLE

The official languages of Puerto Rico are Spanish and English, with Spanish and its Caribbean variants as the dominant language. When my parents attended public school there, English was the medium of instruction for all subjects except Spanish language courses. This was a difficult way to learn since the teachers were rarely native speakers of English and the economy on the island basically functioned in Spanish only. For my siblings and me, Spanish was the medium of instruction and English was taught as a second language subject for 45 minutes each school day. We learned to chant "a" for "acorn" and "a" for "apple" without any understanding of the differences in letter–sound correspondence. We were also mystified by the concept of acorn and apple since there were no oak or apple trees where we lived. My father brought an apple home one day, and the experience of seeing, touching, cutting, and tasting gave the word *apple*, or "manzana," intense meaning followed by subsequent food cravings. It would be years before I would personally pick up acorns on the ground and comprehend that a *bellota* (acorn) was the fruit of *el encino* or *el roble* (varieties of oak trees).

Although the Spanish of Puerto Rico has evolved with many idio-syncrasies that differentiate it from the language variants spoken in other Spanish-speaking countries, we were taught peninsular Spanish. At home and in the streets, however, people used a Spanish influenced by the an-cestral languages of Taínos (indigenous people) and Africans. Interesting-ly, my father was an exception. He had a thirst for complicated poems in peninsular Spanish that he would often read to us. His old tattered poetry books were among the few books we owned when we lived on the island.

Although my father was forced to quit school in 8th grade, he was an avid reader who revered books. Among the texts found in our home there were also political pamphlets shared among adults in the neighbor-hood. The contents of those pamphlets decried the unstable relationship between the United States and Puerto Rico, and were also the same as the messages that blared through speakers atop cars. At the time, I did not know the heated discussions and outcries were about the law forbid-ding the carrying of a Puerto Rican flag, that Puerto Rico's official status was being changed to a Commonwealth, and that this new status was unacceptable to the nationalist movements in Jayuya, Ponce, Mayagüez, Naranjito, Arecibo, Utuado, as well as in San Juan. Even at a tender age, these conversations impressed on me that Spanish was used to discuss poetry, protest injustices, and discuss political principles. English, on the other hand, was the means of communication at work on the military base and a subject to be studied in school. Today, I can observe how the results of English language dominance color everyday language, such as *"Tengo clase*, so *me voy"* ("I have class, so I'm leaving"), rather than the Spanish *entonces* for "therefore." The interjection of English in Spanish discourse has always driven my parents crazy because they grew up in an era where English was imposed and was reserved for particular contexts that had very little tolerance for the mixing of the languages.

MOVING WITH THE MILITARY:
ISLAND AND MAINLAND SCHOOLS

My elementary schooling was interrupted each time my father was trans-ferred from one military post to another. Each move brought its own necessary adjustments to life in and outside of school, and many family dis-cussions regarding different ways of being in island and mainland schools.

I started school at La Academia Santa Monica. The bus from Puerto Nuevo where I lived would take my siblings and me to Avenida Fernán-dez Juncos in Santurce, Puerto Rico, where the school still stands. The school's arches are wide; they grace the outside hallways of the three-storied building. A cross near the roof's center, visible from the surrounding streets, marks the school as Catholic. The garb the priests and nuns wear distinguishes them as followers of St. Augustine.

With classes conducted in Spanish, except one course in English, I learned early about the separation of languages and about the separation of cultures. For example, I was taught that on the U.S. mainland intergenerational relations could be informal, while on the island they could not. I also learned that Catholicism unites people even though vernaculars and social conventions may be different. I felt privileged to attend La Academia Santa Monica. It was a strict and somber beginning of my formal education, presenting all kinds of contradictions.

It was during my years at La Academia that my brother and I were baptized and received our First Holy Communion. We were not baptized as infants because my father was angry with the Catholic Church for demanding an exorbitant stipend to marry my parents. Despite this, however, my *Papá* liked the discipline and values taught by the priests and nuns. This is why my siblings and I attended many Catholic schools during my father's military career.

All the Sisters at La Academia spoke Spanish even though their heritage language may have been English. In this predominantly Spanish-speaking world I met a red-haired, freckled-faced "American" girl. While the teachers and the students in the upper grades could read English, the little American girl in kindergarten seemed to be the only one who pronounced it like a stateside native. I adored and envied her: the way she spoke, the way she looked, even the way she acted—so entitled. She was loud and I was quiet. Her features were light; mine were dark. She was assertive; I was submissive. She was American and I was Puerto Rican. Our only bond was that we were children living in military families, but I did not know that our fathers were serving the *same* nation. I thought she came from another country, even another planet—a place where all people were fair, red-haired, English-speaking, and freckled. It seemed an enviable life.

My red-haired classmate and I passed from kindergarten through 3rd grade together. In 3rd grade we were so excited to read a book in English that was 190 pages long! Our reading book, *These Are Our Friends,* written by Sister M. Marguerite, S.N.D., was part of the Faith and Freedom series whose goal was to teach reading, highlighting the virtues of love, respect, generosity, and helpfulness. David and Ann were the central characters and a very young Sister Jean was their teacher. David and Ann did not wear uniforms at school the way we did. Comprehension questions sometimes were embedded in the stories about their lives. For example, David and Ann's parents gave their children a little white rabbit that eventually ran away. Interestingly, the rabbit talked. "I do not like to eat cookies," he said. "I like green things to eat. I will run away from here." Then the story asked, "Can you guess what kind of green things Little Rabbit wanted?"

Besides comprehension questions, there were also Biblical stories and Catholic doctrine embedded within the stories. For example, one story stated: "Jesus was kind to people when they were hungry. He loves us when we are kind to others, too." These types of messages were important for the spiritual development of children like me. While it seemed nice that the father and mother bought their children a new pet rabbit when Little Rabbit ran away, it also seemed frivolous when I compared it with the needs of my immediate family and my extended family who lived in poverty. I was curious about the life of the characters portrayed in the book, and about the stories about Jesus and his love for everyone, but I was also perplexed by the stories of pets—dogs, cats, rabbits, and birds—whose houses, food, and other needs occupied so much of the family's time and resources. Even more curious was learning about the helpers in their neighborhood—the policemen, firemen, mailmen, and priests. I was mystified that all the jobs were for men, and girls could not be altar girls or priests. However, the book affirmed: "But girls can help God, too. They can be Sisters. Every Sister helps to do God's work. And God needs many more Sisters." In this specific story the message was further elaborated with a prayer that David and Ann repeated every night, "Please, dear God, make many good boys want to be priests. Please, dear God, make many good girls want to be Sisters. Give us many more priests and Sisters to do Your work." I did not know until later about the power of subliminal messages inherent in those readers.

In contrast to the middle-class values represented in the book assigned to my English class, in my 3rd-grade mathematics class in Spanish we used a book whose publisher made efforts to make the word problems culturally relevant. For example, one page showed a black-and-white pencil drawing of a tobacco worker cutting down ripe tobacco with a machete. A review problem for addition read:

"La finca de café"
El café es uno de los productos más importantes de Puerto Rico. Se cultiva en los terrenos montañosos de la Isla. Don José tiene una finca de café. En la finca trabajan muchos obreros. Ramón trabaja con Don José. La semana pasada trabajó tres días. El lunes se ganó $1.50; el martes se ganó $0.85 y el miércoles se ganó $1.10. No pudo trabajar los demás días de la semana debido a la lluvia. ¿Cuánto se ganó Ramón en la semana?

"The coffee plantation"
Coffee is one of the most important products of Puerto Rico. It is cultivated in the mountain regions of the island. Don José has a coffee plantation. Many workers work on the plantation. Ramón works with Don José. Last week he worked three days. On Monday he earned $1.50; on Tuesday he earned $0.85 and on Wednesday he earned $1.10. He could not work the rest of the week because of rain. How much did Ramón earn during that week?

These math problems presented the real economic circumstances of Puerto Rico. As a child I knew my grandfather worked raising and harvesting tobacco, so these culturally relevant word problems provided me a way to understand his world.

LIFE IN THE NORTHEASTERN SEABOARD

In March of my 3rd grade, my father was transferred to North Carolina. Life on the northeastern seaboard in and out of St. Patrick School was a humbling experience. My sister cried and cried during morning prayers because she did not understand English and was subsequently retained in kindergarten. One day soon after our enrollment, my brother suddenly left the school grounds, alarming my parents, school administrators, and the local and military police. Although he was bright, he was impatient when his teacher did not understand what he was trying to say. My *Papito* spent all his free time that spring and summer teaching my brother and me sufficient English to stay at grade level. He also got us a subscription to *Highlights* magazine for children.

It was hard for my parents to live in an all-English environment. *Papito* fared much better than my *Mamita*. They both could understand and read English fairly well but had difficulty producing native-like pronunciation and grammatical forms that could be readily understood. When *Papito* was at work, as the oldest child I was the designated translator for my mother. I often felt inadequate as language broker in places where she needed assistance—the store, the post office, and the doctor's office. I felt little consolation in a foreign land where spoken and unspoken words too often were misunderstood. My excellent grades in English at La Academia Santa Monica were of little value in the English-saturated world where we now lived.

There were many humbling moments. One of the first things I noticed stateside is that few people had red hair. What a disappointment! Another thing I noticed were signs separating Negroes and Whites in certain places, even prohibiting them from drinking from the same water fountains. This segregation scared my mother. She missed San Juan even more because her English reading, writing, and speaking abilities, once effective on the island, were now ineffective in North Carolina. I also noticed that my father wore his U.S. Army uniform even when he was off duty as a way to command respect. This is how we adapted to our new life on the U.S. mainland. In time, it became more acceptable. At school the Sisters paired me up with a little White girl who acted as my language broker. Unfortunately I don't remember her name, but she helped me to become biliterate, *poco a poco*—little by little. In turn, I became a more effective language broker for my mother, the real shining star in my life, who in her role as homemaker had fewer opportunities to develop her English.

LIFE IN THE SOUTHWEST

When my father was transferred to El Paso, Texas, the disquiet that accompanies a move would present new challenges for my family and me. My siblings and I were initially enrolled at a school at Ft. Bliss. Shortly afterward, my father enrolled us at St. Joseph School on Lamar Street. The Sisters of Loretto, with the help of a few lay teachers, ran the school.

One bitter memory I carried for years was inflicted by a Mexican American teacher who made fun of the Puerto Rican Spanish language variant that I used the first day of school. When I asked her, "*¿Dónde puedo encontrar la parada de guaguas?*" ("Where can I find the bus stop?"), she answered, "Speak English. And the correct word for bus is *camión*." I assumed incorrectly that I could use Spanish in school. I also assumed that *guaguas* (buses) referred to the same vehicle in Puerto Rico and in El Paso where there were many Spanish speakers. I was wrong on both counts. At St. Joseph's, in the 1950s, there was a rule that no Spanish was to be used on school grounds, and English-only was strictly upheld. Disobeying the rule was considered a venial sin of disobedience, an offense that had to be confessed. At the age of 10 I had no idea that this woman's Mexican American language variant, *camión*, could be perceived as just as nonstandard as mine. If the accepted Spanish translation for bus is *autobús* or *ómnibus*, then the Mexican variant *camión* should have been as acceptable as my Puerto Rican variant *guagua*.

TRAVELING ON THE BILITERACY HIGHWAY

In Puerto Rico my Spanish heritage language was seen as a right, and an asset. On the mainland, Spanish was seen as a problem to be confessed, if not expunged. Although many Puerto Ricans were stationed at Ft. Bliss, the language ideologies of that era just did not serve our educational needs. Unlike some of our peers who grew up in El Paso, we were not accustomed to English borrowings and frequent language alternations that are awkwardly labeled Spanglish, Tex-Mex, or *pocho*. However, these bilingual-bidialectical youngsters functioned to some degree in both English and Spanish. On the other hand, my siblings and I were unfamiliar with the sophisticated language alternations of our bilingual-bidialectical peers, who knew the appropriate contexts for code switching. Schools encouraged us to lose our Spanish in order to gain English proficiency. This line of reasoning led the Sisters at St. Joseph to advise my parents to stop using Spanish at home. As a result, my parents spoke to us in Spanish and we answered back in English. In terms of biliteracy this meant we persevered in retaining receptive Spanish skills and, over time, lost our productive skills. In many ways the thinking is not different from what teachers think today, that is, bilingualism can be acquired and maintained only sequentially, not simultaneously. Despite prevailing assumptions, my peers in El Paso acquired simultaneous bilingualism, while my siblings and I came to biliteracy in a more sequential manner. Unlike our peers in El Paso, after leaving Puerto Rico we rarely lived in a community with a majority of Spanish speakers. As a consequence, our language development was arrested at various points on the biliteracy highway.

From El Paso, my family traveled to the Vogelweh military complex in Kaiserslautern, Germany, where we attended Department of Defense schools. Instruction was in English and we studied German as a subject on a daily basis. This was in the midst of the Cold War when everyone was consumed by the threat of nuclear weapons, the threat of communism, and the decision to build the 28-mile Berlin Wall that symbolized the Iron Curtain between Western Europe and the Eastern bloc (i.e., Communist or Soviet bloc). While we were in Germany, the U.S. government began sending military advisers to help South Vietnam defend itself against communist North Vietnam. That aid would later expand into a long period of American involvement in Vietnam. As I continued my travel on the biliteracy highway, my languages were enriched as I sang Christmas carols in German and Latin in church, and earned excellent grades in English and other subject areas in junior high school. I also listened to nostalgic Spanish music, particularly *"En Mi Viejo San Juan."* My father played this song over and over again as a response to the passing of his favorite sister. I think my father buried his grief in the lyrics of the song because he could not be with his extended family in his *Borinquen Querido* for the final goodbye to his sister.

During our 3 years in Germany my father was recognized for his unique talents and was promoted to Army Warrant Officer. He had developed skills not only as a bilingual soldier but also as a trilingual one. His third language was Czechoslovakian. In the Cold War era, proficiency in an Eastern bloc language was seen as an important military asset. He also developed important skills related to missiles and associated equipment. I tried not to learn too much about my father's military talents because the danger of war was made real on military bases overseas. Instead, I concentrated on developing my skills in algebra, German, writing, and in track and field athletics.

When our family returned to the U.S. mainland my father was reassigned to a port—San Pedro, California, in the Los Angeles harbor area. This time my younger sisters attended public schools. In 10th grade I attended an all-girls high school, Mary Star of the Sea. My brother attended its counterpart, a new all-boys high school. Sr. Nepomucen was a Sister of the Immaculate Heart of Mary and principal of my school. She was strict but kind. These descriptors fit all the Sisters who taught me. At Mary Star of the Sea, I was not humiliated for any language variant I had, and the only sin that was discouraged was the sin of injustice. I also identified easily with the patronage to Mary, the Mother of Christ. The college-preparatory curriculum meant all the girls could aspire to be scientists, doctors, lawyers, hospital administrators, or superintendents. My parents were also pleased to learn that girls in general, and young ladies of color in particular, had access to opportunities that would not become available to women until the Civil Rights Movement gained momentum. Unfortunately, my father would be transferred after 2 years in San Pedro. We moved to a rural area in the San Fernando valley of California. At that time the Newhall-Saugus area was not very enlightened regarding the roles of young women and men; the social capital I had accumulated at Mary Star of the Sea was not valued. I graduated with my aspirations intact but did not enjoy my last year of K–12 education.

AFTER HIGH SCHOOL . . . *SE HACE EL CAMINO AL ANDAR* [YOU MAKE THE PATH BY WALKING]

The Civil Rights Movement was difficult for my family. I was still in high school when the mass social mobilization, with diverse political agendas from reform to revolution, exhausted every single one of us. To put things in perspective: At the same time that Puerto Rican Young Lords adopted anti-imperialist political programs, my brother was training for infantry encounters in Vietnam. Even in the Catholic Church, priests and nuns took stances to end a war that seemed to promote imperialism. While thousands of Latina/os served in the Tet Offensive with my brother, as a newly recruited member of the Sisters of Immaculate Heart I was at home protesting *against* the war. There were radical transformations of Latina/o identities on the U.S. mainland promoted by *El Movimiento* and liberation theology. I was attracted to these social movements and loved the Vatican II move of the Roman Catholic Church toward ecumenism promoted by Pope John XXIII in 1962. I admired Daniel and Philip Berrigan and Thomas Merton's efforts to create an interfaith coalition against the Vietnam War—the same war in which my brother and future husband experienced physical, psychological, and spiritual wounds. This backdrop provided a bitter paradox of Latina/os dying on U.S. streets in the name of libratory movements, while many of the young men in the U.S. military forces fought for "democracy" in Vietnam. For a very long time my family was divided about the appropriate response to conflicting ideologies—nonviolent resistance or military solutions. The Vietnam War was heart wrenching. My father retired from the U.S. Army and returned to his beloved *Borinquen*; my brother was wounded several times in Vietnam and honored with a Purple Heart.

MEMOIRS OF A *BORICUA* MILITARY CHILD IN THE INTERGENERATIONAL DIASPORA

The Catholic and public schools I attended lacked material resources. In fact, I can't recount a school library. Books were provided by the teacher or borrowed from the local public library in the wider community. There were no Puerto Rican children's literature authors such as Nicholasa Mohr, Judith Ortiz Cofer, Pura Belpré, Lulu Delacre, or Esmeralda Santiago. Our books, for the most part, were the stories of middle-class families living in worlds where children did not worry about the Cold War as I did when my father was stationed in Germany. The biggest struggle for the child protagonist in a story was a misplaced doll, or a pet that ran away, or a spat with a sibling. On one hand, these stories were important to me because my grandmother made my dolls by hand with love and I did lose them. Eventually I had a pet that brought joy in the face of sadness; and I fought with my sister who was favored because she was sickly. On the other hand, the world in those books was solidly White, monocultural, and monolingual; the world in which I lived was not. While I could relate as a child to specific characters in a book, I also felt my family and our lived experiences were for the most part rendered invisible, illegitimate, unlucky, and unpleasant.

There is still so much work to do, so many gaps to fill in the biliteracy road that can provide all of us with the capacity to become fully human in this place called America. In order to address these challenges, as a professor I am grounded in theories that value my personal and professional experiences as a Puerto Rican/DiaspoRican scholar who grew up in a military family. I join many young scholars who use the descriptor Puerto Rican/DiaspoRican to explain what Noel Estrada felt about our Puerto Rican diaspora in the 1940s when he wrote *"En Mi Viejo San Juan."* The various waves of the Puerto Rican diaspora produce unique and important communities in the United States; the emergence of remarkable Puerto Rican music, art, and literature; and the Rican structuring of deficit myths about our capacities as students, families, and locally situated communities throughout America and beyond.

Writing this chapter helped me to remember when I was a high school student attending Mary Star of the Sea. There were days when I would walk from our rental home to this bright spot on the access road where there was a park bench overlooking the ocean in San Pedro, California. I would stare at the waves and watch the sea gulls land and take off from the sand, rocks, or sea. I'd take in deep breaths and reflect on the places my family had seen and imagining all the places I wanted to go. I'd sit out there alone for hours contemplating underneath a canopy of palms. In all that peaceful contemplation, I never imagined I would enter and leave the Sisters of Immaculate Heart of Mary, a religious order so dedicated to nonviolent protest that it was virtually disbanded in the eyes of the Catholic Church by one single man, James Francis Cardinal McIntyre. I never imagined that I would marry a young U.S. Marine whose nightmares of Vietnam would never cease, or that I would go back to school as a graduate student to help César Chávez prepare his lectures for a class on the labor history of California agricultural workers, or that I would become a mother and a grandmother, or that I would become a professor of bilingual-bicultural studies. On that bench by the ocean I didn't realize the journey toward Mi Viejo San Juan would take decades to actually materialize. But I did return—first, to bring my firstborn to meet his grandparents, then to take my grandsons to the place where I was born. Now as a professor, I go regularly to work with professors on the island who are also dedicated to cultivating the linguistic and cultural resources that maintain biliterate lives. I have a deep sense of gratitude and give thanks to those people big and small that have supported me, for holding me up, for helping me return to the *Borinquen Querido* that is my legacy.

As I look back at my past and look ahead into my children's and my grandchildren's future, I am again amazed at how far we've come, yet how much further we have to go. What I learned in 5th grade at St. Joseph School, and deliberate now, is how cruel we can be to one another when as Latina/os we are not made aware of our intragroup differences in language, history, and traditions. Not knowing the individual stories behind our efforts to retain our bilingualism and biliteracy makes us vulnerable to divisions. Our diverse stories provide the foundation for coalition building and achieving solidarity. The power of our stories of resilience against all odds is what unites us and makes this book a singular contribution for generations to come.

CHAPTER 11

Pedro, Peter, Pete, and Pito

Pedro Pedraza

Upon entering school, Pedro would begin to understand the important connection between his name and his multiple identities. Each derivation of his name would link him to people and places on the mainland (New York City) and on the island of Puerto Rico that would contribute to his development as a bilingual, bicultural, and biliterate person. With the increasingly diverse student population in schools, this chapter reminds us of the importance of respecting student names; that changing them to make it easier for teachers is an insult to their families. It underscores the idea that each of us enjoys multiple identities that come with corresponding discourses, and illustrates the fact that maintaining heritage languages is an on-going struggle for linguistically diverse students in U.S. schools.

On the first day of kindergarten my teacher introduced me to the class as "Peter." The very next day, my mother marched to school to inform her that my name was Pedro and that she preferred the teacher address me as Pedro, not "Peter." Ironically, my mother called me Peter at home to distinguish me from my father, Pedro Senior. As a matter of fact, it didn't much matter to her that the neighborhood kids called me Peter, and more often, "Pete." In those days, teachers were famous for translating Spanish names into English or inventing new ones. My parents had named me Pedro and only they had the right to change it. Perhaps this is what my mother was trying to convey to my teacher.

On my first visit to Puerto Rico in the summer before kindergarten, another name was added to my repertoire of names. My extended family on the island nicknamed me Pito, because a young cousin couldn't pronounce Pedrito. To this day that's what they call me. Pedro, Peter, Pete, and Pito, each of these names was (and continues to be) associated with my multiple identities and with the various social relationships I have with others. They represent my connections with the diverse linguistic communities with whom I interacted as I was growing up.

LANGUAGE CONTEXT AT HOME

At home my mother spoke to me in English; my father in Spanish. I answered and spoke to both in English. My parents tried their best to expose me to Spanish outside the home. Until I was 8 or 9 years old, for example, we attended the First Spanish Baptist Church of New York City in East Harlem, or *El Barrio,* as the neighborhood was known to the Puerto Rican community. At this church, religious services were conducted in Spanish, helping my receptive skills, but this didn't last long. When we moved to a low-income public housing project on the West Side of Manhattan, we switched to the Good Shepherd Faith Presbyterian Church. There, the majority of the congregation was African American. The small group of Spanish-speaking parishioners were mostly 1st-generation adults, with whom I had little in common, so I stopped attending the separate services. Instead, I participated in Sunday school instruction in English with my African American friends. This change eliminated my only formal access to spoken Spanish outside the home. At school and in the neighborhood I spoke primarily English. This left only a small number of older adults from the island with whom I interacted in Spanish in the community.

FIRST VISIT TO THE ISLAND

As mentioned earlier, at age 5, I visited Puerto Rico for the first time. By propeller plane the flight took 8 hours. On our arrival around 6 a.m., a crowd of relatives awaited us at the airport. It took all day to reach my grandparents' farm outside Las Piedras, my father's hometown. What made the trip to the farm extra long was that our relatives stopped at the home of *every* kin along the way to show off the *"Americanitos"* in the family. Initially, my Puerto Rican relatives called me Pedro, or Pedrito, but quickly switched to Pito.

My grandparents lived in a small, rural, largely Spanish monolingual community with limited exposure to English media. I would learn much later that soon after Puerto Rico became a U.S. territory, the federal government imposed English language classes in all island schools. This bold attempt to coerce school children to adopt English was a major source of contention for the islanders. At the time, the language currency was Spanish and Puerto Ricans had little to no exposure to the colonizer's language. My family had little use for English; at least, that's how it seemed to me at the time. Looking back, I see that their reluctance or refusal to switch to English was a symbol of their resistance to English hegemony.

During my 3 months in Puerto Rico, I began speaking more Spanish and gradually lost most of my English fluency. Getting to know my father's family on the island was a means of discovering my Puerto Rican roots. It was also a whole new experience for me, my brother, and my mother, who were born and raised in New York City and had never been, or lived, on a farm before.

On the first night at my grandparent's farm I was terrorized by a small pig running through the middle of the house. The next day I saw a headless chicken running around the yard and discovered that we were eating it for dinner! However strange these events seemed, 3 months later I left Puerto Rico, realizing how much I loved the farm. For a little city kid like me, Puerto Rico was a paradise—in spite of the inconveniences of mosquito nets, the outhouse, the chamber pot under the bed, and warm cow's milk. Although each of these new experiences took some getting used to, I came to enjoy it all—the huge extended family, their warmth and happy chatter, and especially my grandmother's cooking. Her meals were always prepared with fresh fruits, vegetables, and other produce grown on the farm.

At the end of that vacation, I remember the tension I felt returning to school in New York City. My teacher was impatient as I attempted to recover my English fluency. I felt hostility even toward any acknowledgment of my Spanish skills—to me a confusing resentment bordering on complete rejection of my newly acquired Spanish fluency.

However, I'd retained enough English receptive skills that I could still trade places at dinnertime with Michael, the son of the Italian family who lived next door. Michael loved rice and beans, and I, spaghetti. Instead of fighting with their sons to eat dinner, our mothers set up this exchange. It was easier to accommodate us than put up with our protests.

I remember my friends' fascination with my changed and changing persona—a fascination they demonstrated in their acceptance of my re-emerging English-speaking identity. Linguistically, it was a confusing time for me; my elation at knowing Spanish wavered outside of familial contexts and English soon dominated, reducing my use of Spanish to limited domains.

A LANGUAGE U-TURN

By the time I graduated from junior high school, my language proficiency had made a complete reversal: Now I was an English-dominant speaker with passive ability in Spanish. Although I could understand Spanish, I could not speak it fluently. In my early teenage years, when peer pressure is intense, my friends were 2nd- and 3rd-generation Puerto Ricans like myself. Although we had various degrees of Spanish fluency, we preferred to speak English. Years later I came to understand that we spoke a nonstandard form of New York City working-class English strongly influenced by Black Vernacular English.

Coincidentally, in graduate school I would end up working on sociolinguistic research examining nonstandard forms of NYC English with William Labov, a well-known sociolinguist at Columbia University. Like African American youth, my Puerto Rican buddies and I also used "sounding," or playing the dozens. We used the form "be" as in "he be sleeping late on Saturday mornings," as part of our teenage discourse. When the conversation shifted to Latino music, we switched to Spanish. NYC salsa was emerging, and the *salseros* sung in Spanish. Occasionally, I used Spanish as a sign of respect, to accommodate monolingual elders and new arrivals within our peer group. I am not sure how aware I was of the diverse language vernaculars I was using in English and Spanish at the time, but I remember it was cool to flex Black Vernacular English in church and shift to a Walter Cronkite-like-English, a more academic and standard form. We used a range of dialects, or dialectic features, within our two languages, which we manipulated in various social contexts and with various speakers in our surroundings. These manipulations reflected our expertise in controlling our two linguistic systems and the various forms of discourse at our disposal. These mirrored our multiple identities and the norms of the speech community. As Ana Celia Zentella, a noted Puerto Rican sociolinguist, points out—that's the beauty of being bilingual.

My junior high school included an internationally diverse, poor, immigrant, working-class student body. In my 7th-grade class, for example, there were Greek, Italian, Chinese, Puerto Rican, African American, Irish, and other Latino students. One of our English teachers used to emphasize how unique we were to be right next to the Broadway theater district with such an international mix of kids. We knew the neighborhood as "Hell's Kitchen" and took advantage of the theater district to peek at burlesque shows and eat lunch at the Horn & Hardart Automat, where we became experts at beating the vending machines by getting two selections for one coin in each slot. But, as much as we tried, we never really got in to see any of the live shows.

BECOMING BILINGUAL AND BILITERATE

Before starting high school, I returned to Puerto Rico for a second time. My mother stayed in New York so I was by myself on this trip. This time I began to develop and solidify a more permanent Spanish proficiency, speaking it with more confidence. As a result of being an avid Yankee baseball fan, I even learned to read Spanish that summer. On the island, I quickly realized that the only way I could follow my team was through Spanish language media. This fact forced me to read about the Yankees in the sports section of a local Spanish newspaper I would pick up at a barbershop a few times a week. Not surprisingly, the barbers were devoted Roberto Clemente fans. They followed his day-by-day career. At the barbershop I would listen to their daily commentary on the players, teams, and races.

Many things were different on this trip to Puerto Rico. For one thing, I was now a teenager and my extended family was now residing in the center of town instead of at the farm. Both factors enabled me to experience many aspects of Puerto Rican life on my own. Also, there was no alternative but to hone my Spanish skills because I was immersed in a community of mostly Spanish speakers. There was so much to experience: horseback riding through the sugar cane and pineapple fields, bathing in the still uncontaminated streams, swimming in the clear blue waters of the white sandy beaches, and listening to *Cortijo y Su Combo* with Ismael Rivera. I discovered Latin music from the island traditions of *bomba* and *plena* on the radio and from the mid-day TV variety shows (siesta was still the custom), and in the town's only dance club, *El Cerezo*. I also spent Saturday evenings *tirando flores* (flirting, showering compliments) as we watched young girls circle the plaza. Once, I even accompanied my cousin for a *serenata a su novia* (a serenade to his girlfriend). Another pastime was hanging out at the plaza calling out the make, model, and year of cars driving by. Much to my advantage and growing curiosity, at that time there was no drinking age in Puerto Rico. That was one of the best summers of my life.

THE AMSTERDAM HOUSES:
A MULTIETHNIC, MULTILINGUAL ENVIRONMENT

At the end of the summer, I returned to New York and back to my home in the projects, officially named the Amsterdam Houses. The Amsterdam Houses were among the first half dozen or so public housing developments built by the New York City Housing Authority, which today still administers 345 such developments. Until the late 1950s and early 1960s, these houses were situated in the middle of a neighborhood of tenement buildings. In those years an urban development project called for demolishing the tenements to make room for the now-famous Lincoln Center Cultural Complex. The blocks surrounding the projects housed Irish families on 60th to 62nd Streets, Puerto Ricans between 63rd and 64th Streets, and Italians between 65th and 68th Streets—working-class communities that became the sets for the filming of "West Side Story."

The Amsterdam Houses provided a place to live for multiethnic working-class communities. By the end of the 1960s and through the 1970s, the projects were transformed into an almost exclusively Black and Puerto Rican population—the product of two early- to mid-20th-century migrations from Puerto Rico and the deep South.

People who lived and grew up in the Amsterdam Houses during that era felt (and still feel) a strong sense of community, a special bond with the place—so much so, that there is an annual reunion every summer. On August 2, 2004, the *New York Times* published an article about these reunions under the title, "The Neighborhood Ties That Still Bind: Children from a Postwar Project Revisit the Time of Their Lives" (Kilgannon, 2004). Former residents from all walks of life and from every corner of the United States turned up to eat, drink, dance, play softball or stickball, reminisce, and reconnect. Those of us who lived in the Amsterdam Houses shared with, helped, and defended one another. There were three gangs in the projects, two Puerto Rican and one African American. Each group had an understanding about their respective territorial boundaries. This understanding helped prevent conflicts between us, but when people from the outside tried to enter, all three gangs met them. Of course, this never precluded individual intra- or interethnic conflict. We all mixed socially at the community center dances and special events.

During the warm summer months the Amsterdam projects bustled with activity. On any summer night you could walk through the projects and see or hear children playing marbles, checkers, tops, and other popular children's games. Teens and adults would be engaged in a variety of card games: whist, blackjack, dice, rummy, and casino favorites, or pool, ping pong, and table hockey at the community center during the school year.

The neighborhood was also teeming with rich cultural and musical diversity. DoWop groups sang a capella *plena*; Latino musicians improvised with mailboxes, cans, *guiros, rumba,* and *guanguanco* with *congas.* Well-known Puerto Rican *plena* singer Mon Rivera and famous African American jazz musician Thelonious Monk lived in the community. Posters were plastered around the community announcing Latin dances at the nearby Palladium or Riverside Plaza with Machito, Tito Puente and Rodriguez, and Joe Cuba (other favorite Puerto Rican musicians), or jazz with Count Basie, Duke Ellington, Sarah Vaughan, Ella Fitzgerald, and others who performed at the Savoy, Cotton Club, and Audubon ballroom uptown. *El Estudio* movie theater was also nearby, featuring all the latest Spanish language, Mexican films with Pedro Infante, Libertad LaMarque, Cantinflas, Pedro Armendariz, and other Mexican movie stars. Although we resisted when parents and grandparents dragged us youngsters to see these movies, the films provided us exposure and continuing connection to the Spanish language.

My high school, Charles Evans Hughes, was much farther downtown than my junior high and drew students from a much wider area: Harlem, the upper West Side, Chelsea/Hell's Kitchen, and the projects. Although it was a "majority minority" school, my academic track put me in classes with mostly White students. In the mornings, I'd go to school with my neighborhood friends but not see them except during gym and lunch periods. At the end of the day, I would join them again for the trip home. The school held about 3,000 or so students; my freshman class had around 1,000. Of these, only about 200 would graduate and approximately 50 would go on to some form of postsecondary education. The drop-out rate was staggering even then. The dominant language in all of these contexts was, of course, English, but not the standard variety by any means.

CONTRADICTORY EXPERIENCES

I started working when I was 12 years old, selling newspapers: *Daily News, Daily Mirror, N.Y. Post, Journal American,* and, on occasion, a few *Herald Tribunes* and the *New York Times* door to door, Monday through Friday. On Saturdays, I'd go down to the bars on Broadway, where the clients were mostly Irish, hoping to hit on drunks who would pay a buck to five bucks for a nickel paper. When I got my working papers (a legal permit to work under age), I started delivering for a local pharmacy and supermarket, where I ended up as a cashier.

In high school I worked at an East Side flower shop making deliveries after school. There, I met Jason, a young African American, who worked full time. He was always talking about "Brother Malcolm." Frequently, Jason would get into heated discussions with an older, southern Black man who had worked at the flower shop for many years. Each had a different view of Brother Malcolm. One saw a troublemaker; the other a liberator. My own church congregation did not view Malcolm X's ideas as a source of inspiration, although members did credit him for speaking out against injustices. Due to my religious affiliation and influence, Malcolm being a Muslim, I tended to agree with the old man. One day, at the end of our last deliveries, Jason took me by 125th and Lenox on our way home so we could hear Malcolm X talk. I was amazed at how many police officers were there to contain the crowd. We couldn't see Malcolm X well from where we stood but I had a few glimpses of him. We listened for a while, but I left before it was over. I went home, not wanting to like Malcom X, but I was unable to shake the logic of his arguments concerning injustice, intolerance, inequality, and human rights, including the importance of pride and respect for one's culture.

Despite this, I still had conservative leanings. On two occasions African American students at my high school organized protests, boycotts, and walkouts over civil injustices. Although I sympathized with them, I could not support their methods of protest. I did not see how jeopardizing my education by missing classes could resolve injustices. All my friends took the days off; they thought I was crazy not to. It didn't much matter what I thought about the issue. It's odd that my Puerto Rican identity seemed to keep me on the sidelines of this other real-life drama taking place in the larger English-speaking minority community. These two worlds would eventually merge in my politically active postgraduate period.

EMERGING POLITICAL AND CULTURAL IDENTITY

It was largely through the efforts of Aspira, a Puerto Rican youth development organization founded by Antonia Pantoja, that I was motivated to consider college. A deacon at my church told me about scholarships at Occidental College and helped me apply. He had raised money to pay for college application fees as part of his campaign to get some church youth into college. Since it was free, I thought, why not?

I wanted to leave New York because I knew staying near home presented many distractions and I would never finish my coursework. Thanks to a Rockefeller minority scholarship, I went off to Los Angeles, California, to enroll in Occidental College. The irony didn't elude me that this was the height of the Civil Rights Movement and I was the first and only Puerto Rican undergraduate student at Occidental—and I was a conservative at that. Occidental was a predominantly White, wealthy institution that could afford to pay chambermaids to change our bed linens once a week, now a long gone practice. Looking back, I realize that the minority scholarship recipients were intended to integrate Occidental. (Some years later, Occidental would enroll a now-famous student by the name of Barack Obama. Today Occidental has a student body comprising one third Latinos and African Americans.)

The year was 1964 and I found myself with a majority of Republican students who, in a university straw poll, voted overwhelmingly for Barry Goldwater for President. In the actual elections, the Democrat, Lyndon Baines Johnson, won by a landslide. From the beginning, a majority of my White peers opposed Johnson's civil rights agenda and the War on Poverty. They argued that there was no need for either one; that people were poor because they were lazy and didn't want to work. I was stunned by their ignorance regarding the economic struggles of ordinary people and about the rampant discrimination against minorities across the country.

It was hard for me to reconcile the fact that I was attending an institution of higher learning, a uniquely privileged one, supposedly dedicated to the pursuit of truth, but instead I was encountering profound ignorance about minorities and perceptions based largely on stereotypes and prejudicial views emanating from an openly racist ideology.

I engaged in heated arguments with students that often left me angry and frustrated. This period radicalized me. Being away from my Puerto Rican community and finding myself alone made me keenly aware of the social inequities in our society and my own previous lack of attention to them in New York. So I joined the United Mexican American Students, the Black Students Union, and Students for a Democratic Society, which were all involved in social justice agendas. My involvement in these organizations not only made me more knowledgeable of the issues, but it also gave me a sense of pride in my own cultural identity as a Puerto Rican and as a member of a minority group, which I now viewed as an asset. My response to social inequities was visceral, a response that continues to motivate me to this day.

I discovered, and ended, the false dichotomy I had set up between my Spanish-speaking world and the political destiny of Puerto Ricans. I began to see important connections between political activism and my academic endeavors as a way to work for social justice. Eventually, this led to an academic career at a research institute, *El Centro de Estudios Puertorriqueños*, where I became an activist scholar/educator, and social scientist. "Pedro's" persona dominates in this arena.

SOLIDIFYING MY MULTIPLE IDENTITIES

The wide range and rich diversity of experiences I have enjoyed throughout my life in New York, Puerto Rico, and elsewhere have all contributed to solidifying my multiple identities as Pedro, Peter, Pete, and Pito. They have contributed to my development of bilingualism and biliteracy, two resources that play an important role in my life as a professional.

Growing up in New York City among so much cultural and linguistic diversity required openness and flexibility in accommodating different contexts and situations. I witnessed historical social, cultural, and political events unfolding right before my eyes or in close proximity to my community: the height of Latino music, the jazz renaissance, and the turmoil of the Civil Rights Movement. Being at the right place, at the right time, provided me a front row seat to the emerging careers of many famous Americans in music, athletics, and politics. That adaptability, which is part and parcel of being bilingual and bicultural, turned out to be a valuable asset for me. My lifelong education began in schools and neighborhoods that mirrored the racial diversity of the "united nations" and served as a precursor of the racial, ethnic, cultural, and linguistic diversity that would spread to the rest of the country. In the end, living and breathing in all those varied social contexts finally enabled my social consciousness to seep through.

Overcoming the Odds—
Lessons Across Generations

María de la Luz Reyes

The collection of counterstories in this book give voice to resilient Latina/o youth (Delgado & Stefancic, 2001; Yosso, 2006) who managed to outfox a powerful system intent on transforming them into something less than what they were capable of becoming. Their personal stories echo the sentiment of many an immigrant who often wonders why the price of becoming American is so high. Ray Suarez (2007) tells of one such immigrant who came to the United States and asked him: "*¿Por qué sería bueno convertirme en menos de lo que soy para hacerme un americano? Yo he probado esta cosa nueva, del inglés, pero no significa que tenga que dejar lo que era cuando llegué.*" ("Why would it be good to transform myself into less than what I am to become an American? I have tried that new thing, English, but that doesn't mean that I have to discard what I was when I arrived.") (p. xiii).

Although it is illogical to argue that bilingualism is less valuable than monolingualism, that is precisely the idea that schools promote when they work to eradicate and transform bi(multi)lingual students into English monolinguals and tout this conversion as a superior model.

A majority of Latinos have a strong attachment to Spanish; they view it as a key aspect of their identity. Gloria Anzaldua (1987) described the indissoluble connection between a person and her language when she proclaimed, "I am my language" (p. 59). Valdés (1997) claims that Spanish "has served as a shared treasure, a significant part of a threatened heritage, and a secret language" (p. 393). In a similar vein, González (2001) contends that the strong link between language and emotion "is one of the ties that bind children to a sense of heritage" (p. xix). Language, then, is a primary means by which people establish their identity (Street, 1988). Rejection of Spanish in schools has taught Puerto Ricans and Chicanos that "there is no language without politics" (Zentella, 1997, p. 14).

Chicana/o and Puerto Rican students of a bygone era, much like the immigrant interviewed by Suarez (2007), contested the notion that "less was more." They held on to "the words they had" and refused to relinquish their Spanish in exchange for academic success. Although they did not set out to oppose the educational system, when schools required singular allegiance to English, the unreasonableness of that demand compelled them to push back (Halcón, personal communication, April 1, 2010). Defying the system made it possible for them to become biliterate. Students learned to take calculated risks to subvert oppressive school practices, even developing a "thick skin" that helped them endure injurious attacks on their linguistic, ethnic, and class identities. Their rejection of dominant ideology paid off. Today, these authors are recognized scholars and noted leaders in education and in Latino communities across the country. As they moved through the grades, they continued to challenge an old, but implacable, view that Spanish was detrimental to their academic success (Crawford, 1992).

While still in their formative years, these Latinos were successful in eluding a powerful socializing institution that stripped millions of other linguistic minority students of their language. Between the lines, the authors described how they developed expert skills in adaptive and oppositional strategies. Like those of other minoritized groups (González, 2001), their actions and choices revealed a hopefulness that kept "them going, struggling and surviving, albeit precariously, *against the odds* [emphasis added] and without the support of the society to which they belonged" (Taylor & Dorsey-Gaines, 1988, p. 192). Equally important, the stories demonstrate that even among the most economically deprived families, Latino parents are interested in their children's education and have the capacity and desire to help them. Parents can tap into their funds of knowledge to impart values and social practices that form the basis for language and literacy development. We learn from the authors' narratives that mothers were directly engaged in numerous social practices that supported literacy: conversing with their children in Spanish; telling oral stories, rhymes, and proverbs (see Reyes, this volume); teaching the Spanish alphabet, phonics, and syllabication (see Bartolomé, this volume); teaching writing (see Valadez, this volume); involving their children in letter–sound correspondence and other functional writing (see Arvizu and Bartolomé, this volume); taking them to libraries (see Nieto, this volume), and promoting Spanish literacy with popular reading materials such as *novelas, fotonovelas,* and *revistas* (see Arvizu, Bartolomé, Balderrama, González, and Halcón, this volume). In some instances, extended family members and close associates also participated in reading stories or teaching basic elements of literacy (see Arvizu, Balderrama, Bartolomé, González, and Mercado, this volume). Sharing oral readings with loved ones frequently imbues the event with emotional power, leaving a lasting and positive association with literacy (Galindo, 2001) and with the language of the text.

Latino fathers, often depicted as disengaged in their children's learning, were, in fact, equally involved in supporting their children's education. Some read scripture (see González, this volume), others poetry (see Fránquiz, this volume), or daily newspapers, engaging their family in critical discussions of current events (see Fránquiz and Valadez, this volume). Still others served as language models for their children (see Bartolomé, Halcón, and Pedraza, this volume) and introduced their children to the public library (see Halcón and Nieto, this volume). While the majority of these social practices took place in Spanish, they laid a strong foundation for English literacy. Street (1988) concurs that literacy in one language supports it in another language, suggesting that differences between dominant (English) and nondominant (Spanish) languages are merely different points on the oral and literate continuum. Language and literacy in one language often have a positive transfer effect in another (Cummins, 1981). Much like Heath (1983), Hornberger (2003) points out that differences between oral and literate cultures, or between one language and another, are not as critical as "which literacies most closely resemble those of the school" (p. 12).

The educational experiences of past generations of Latinos mirror the current challenges facing young Latino students. They bring to light the schools' failure to recognize and utilize Latino communities' funds of knowledge as important resources for learning and literacy acquisition (González, Moll, & Amanti, 2005; Moll, 1992).

NO SINGLE EXPLANATION

Despite the presence of recurring themes across narratives, there is no single, or simple, explanation for how individuals managed to succeed academically, how they retained a native language that was under constant attack, or how they emerged literate in English and Spanish. This revelation underscores the fact that Latinos are exceedingly heterogeneous and that their lives do not fit or reflect essentialized and stereotypical elements often used to describe them (González, 2001).

While all authors displayed a better than average sociolinguistic and academic intelligence in both their pursuit of knowledge and their contestation of English hegemony, their responses to school conditions varied widely, resulting in different paths to biliteracy. Given this, it is difficult to identify neat, predictable patterns in their biliteracy development, their maintenance of bilingualism, and their identity formation.

Hornberger's (2003) framework, the "continua of biliteracy," is a useful tool in understanding the complexity of biliteracy. According to the model, all interrelated biliterate contexts, including individual and media-related factors, lie along the continua. Monoliteracy and biliteracy, for example, are merely different points on a continuum, not polar opposite competencies. At any given time, an individual can occupy a different point on each continuum, depending on the social context, interlocutors, and other aspects of an event. Movement along a continuum is fluid and highly dependent on the individual and the various inextricably linked contexts. This suggests, for example, that while all authors may be biliterate, one individual may occupy a more academically biliterate point on the continua than others. In the following section intergroup and intragroup similarities and differences, as well as emerging themes, are discussed.

SIMILARITIES AND DIFFERENCES

Without exception, all authors were children of poor, working-class families living in minority or low-income communities, or ethnic enclaves. Despite this, individuals responded in unique ways to the sociopolitical and sociohistorical contexts in which they found themselves. Prohibition of Spanish in school, for example, was equally applicable to Chicanos and Puerto Ricans, but it seemed to pose a more overt threat to Chicanos than to Puerto Ricans. One reason for this might be that Chicanos in the Southwest functioned in a binary world where unequal power relations between Whites and Chicanos were more apparent than the differences between Whites and all other ethnic groups who attended schools alongside Puerto Ricans.

LANGUAGE AND POWER

Because power and language are so tightly linked, Carson (as cited in Hornberger, 2003) argues that language is a means to exert power and "language is a vehicle for indentifying, manipulating, and changing power relations" (p. 38). Crawford (1992) also found that much of the fervor behind the English-only movement was motivated by the fear of losing power; the dominant group believed that maintenance of non-English languages was a kind of minority ruse for taking over the country.

The Case of Chicana/os

The critical mass of Chicanos in schools and the proximity of Texas and California to the Mexican border presented a potential threat to the pre-eminence of English. The conspicuousness of Spanish among Chicanos continually disrupted the primacy of English on school campuses, giving teachers license to take on the role of "language police," freely meting out punishment for minor infractions of the ban on Spanish, even in instances when the translation of instructions would have been beneficial to a teacher's overall success with her students. I concur with Balderrama (this volume), who argues that exerting one's bilingual rights in oral discourse is more political than demonstrating one's biliteracy because the former is viewed by xenophobes as more confrontational, and the latter more of a private act.

The Case of Puerto Ricans

In contrast to Chicanos, Puerto Ricans lived in highly diverse communities and generally attended schools in large urban cities with many other ethnic minorities (Mercado, Nieto, and Pedraza, this volume). While schools in the Northeast also banned Spanish, the ban applied to the use of *all* non-English languages: Italian, Greek, Russian, Yiddish, and others, diminishing the singular assault on Spanish. This is not to say that Puerto Ricans did not feel alienated in classrooms, that their Spanish was not stigmatized, or that they did not yearn to be like others or to be accepted for who they were (see Fránquiz, Mercado, and Nieto, this volume). The intense need to belong, to be like others, sometimes manifested itself in a rejection of Spanish and of their cultural identity, and even feelings of shame over their parents—feelings and attitudes that later would be "recalibrated" and reversed (see Nieto, this volume).

Response to Punishment

But even within groups, responses varied widely. Punishment for speaking Spanish was a recurring theme among Chicanos, but responses were dependent on individuals' personality and temperament, each taking a distinctive twist. Concepción Valadez (this volume), for example, felt humiliated and often cried, while at the same time she built resilience. Steven Arvizu (this volume) wrote his sentence, "I will not use Spanish in school," 500 times, taking his punishment in stride and his Spanish language underground. John Halcón (this volume) retaliated against unreasonable punishment for speaking Spanish and, in defiance, refused to continue as the principal's translator.

Puerto Rican authors did not mention punishment for speaking Spanish, except for Fránquiz (this volume), who was punished for speaking Spanish in a Catholic school in El Paso, Texas, where a violation of the rule also was considered a venial sin, a double whammy infraction in heaven and on earth. Puerto Rican students suffered the effects of language discontinuity between home and school. All contributors mentioned incidences when their dialect was disparaged in school. Even when they returned to Puerto Rico, native islanders criticized their language variety. One critic even portrayed the language variety of New York Puerto Ricans as "a bastardization of the [Spanish] language" (see Mercado, this volume).

THE PRACTICE OF NAME CHANGING

In addition to the attempts to eradicate Spanish in schools, there was also the common practice of translating Spanish names into English or fabricating new ones for others (see Halcón, Pedraza, and Reyes, this volume). Changing a student's name was another attempt to weaken the connection to students' cultural identities; it was part of the Americanization process. While individual teachers may have done this with no malicious intent, the practice was part of the overall goal of Americanization of ethnic minorities, and of shifting their allegiance from Spanish to English.

MULTIPLE PATHS TO BILITERACY

The different paths to biliteracy were highly dependent on personality, agency, and the sociopolitical and sociohistorical contexts in which individuals lived and where they attended school. These findings are consistent with those of González (2001), Hornberger (2003), Maguire (1999),

Moll & Dworin (1996), Ramírez (1994), Reyes (2001), and Tse (2001). There were no predictable patterns even among Chicanos living in close proximity to the Mexican border, where one might expect similarities given the large population of Spanish speakers along the border. Josué González (this volume), for example, attended schools in South Texas where students and (many) teachers were Chicanos. It is probably the case that, despite the ban on Spanish, his teachers employed familiar interactional and instructional styles that matched those of their students. In an environment where there were ample professional role models, biliteracy was easier to attain. For John Halcón (this volume), who lived less than 30 miles from Mexicali, Mexico, White and Chicano communities were divided along economic lines, accentuating the subordinate status of Chicanos. Few Chicanos occupied positions of power. Most of his teachers were White, forcing him to navigate his way through school, sometimes adapting, but often fighting back against attempts at the erasure of his native language, a language his mother insisted he learn. María Balderrama (this volume), who lived about 10 miles from Mexicali, attended a small rural school in a post-*Brown v. Board of Education* and post-Civil Rights Act era, had more positive school experiences than Halcón. The difference was not only the sociopolitical and sociohistorial context of the day, but also was the fact that she was one of only a handful of *mexicanos* in her school, so she posed no threat to English dominance. Given that she attended elementary school in the early 1960s, her teacher appeared to be more sensitive to the different linguistic needs of her pupils, and appointed a bilingual peer to help her with English. But this was not the case throughout Balderrama's school years.

Despite these differences, the authors provide important lessons of survival; they lay bare their instincts to survive a system that worked against them rather than for them.

CONTRIBUTING FACTORS TO BILITERACY

The Vitality of Spanish

A key contributing factor to the maintenance of Spanish was the vitality of the language in the narrators' homes and their communities (Ramírez, 1994). Although Spanish was a "marked language" in schools and in the larger English-speaking community (Fishman, 1989), it was the primary means of communication in most Chicano and Puerto Rican homes.

Tse (2001) argues that a mother's use of Spanish, and her encouragement (even insistence) that her children speak and maintain their heritage language, is of particular importance in sustaining the native language (see also Halcón, this volume). That seems to be the case in the authors' narratives. With the exception of one author (see Pedraza, this volume), the authors' mothers employed Spanish as the primary means of communication with their children, contributing to the robustness of Spanish in the home and in the barrios where they lived.

In some cases, English was utilized alongside Spanish, with one parent assuming the role of Spanish speaker, the other of English speaker, continually exposing their children to both systems of communication (see Bartolomé, Halcón, and Pedraza, this volume). Bartolomé and Halcón matched the language of the speakers, reinforcing both their languages. Pedraza, however, spoke English to both parents.

Without the vitality of Spanish in Latino communities, it would have been difficult for Chicano and Puerto Rican youth to sustain their heritage language, as has been the case for other linguistic minorities whose native language lacks vigor (Tse, 2001).

Parents' Roles in Literacy Development

Mothers were instrumental in teaching, encouraging, and assisting their children in becoming literate in Spanish. Although they did not have the financial means to purchase books, they provided their children inexpensive popular cultural magazines (*revistas*), *novelas*, and *fotonovelas* (see Bartolomé, this volume, for a fuller description) or, in some cases, took them to the public library to check out books (see Nieto, this volume). Some mothers took an active role in teaching reading and writing (see Bartolomé and Valadez, this volume). Other mothers simply exposed their children to *novelas*, or set aside time for their children to read *novelas* (see Halcón, this volume). Still other children read *novelas* alone (see Arvizu, this volume), with friends (see González, this volume), or with extended family members (see Balderrama and Mercado, this volume). Sharing *novelas* was often a social event and a social practice (see especially Balderrama, Bartolomé, González, and Halcón, this volume). Fathers also helped foster an interest and love of reading as was the case with Halcón and his father (this volume).

Cultural Agency

Individual agency and motivation explain, in part, why some students become biliterate and others do not (Dworin, 2003; Maguire, 1999; Moll & Dworin, 1996). Schools and classrooms are not neutral spaces, however; they embody and project a particular ethos that is shaped by a teacher's political ideology (Bartolomé & Balderrama, 2001), often weakening a student's agency. Teachers' attitudes can either enable or disable students' discourse values and preferences and shift the direction they will take in learning, maintaining, or discarding their heritage language (Maguire, 1999). Despite their teachers' attempts to censor Spanish, authors in this volume demonstrated strong cultural agency in their personal determination to remain bilingual and biliterate. They exerted effort to learn and use oral and written Spanish outside of school. Many used Spanish as a means of communication with their peers, further ensuring its verve within their inner circles (Tse, 2001). Living in Spanish-speaking barrios and communities presented potential access to Spanish print.

The Role of Churches

Churches, particularly the Catholic Church in Latino communities, have played a major role in sustaining ethnic minority languages (Pak, 2003; Reyes, 2008; San Miguel, 1987; Tse, 2001). Dating back to the establishment of Mexican missions, the Catholic Church permitted and encouraged priests to use Spanish for religious services as a way to increase membership among Mexicans, and as a way to facilitate conversion to Catholicism (Reyes, 2008). Catholic, Baptist, Methodist, and other Christian churches have been instrumental in sustaining Spanish in Latino communities in the United States (Pak, 2003; see also González, Pedraza, and Reyes, this volume). For children of devout church attendees, frequent exposure to religious texts, such as the Bible, scripture passages, prayer books, missals, and hymnals, has served as a helpful tool for acquiring Spanish literacy (Galindo, 2001; see also Reyes, this volume). When churches conduct religious services in a language ordinarily depicted as inferior, this has the effect of elevating the status of a stigmatized language to a privileged position, and inverting the power dynamics within the church context (Galindo, 2001; Pak, 2003). While English may have a pre-eminent position in the larger social milieu, churches serving Latino and other ethnic communities historically have served as safe havens for minority languages, helping to sustain Spanish. In addition, use of heritage languages in churches has helped affirm cultural practices and social identities (see Reyes, this volume).

The Role of Spanish Language Films

In an era when few Latinos owned televisions, Mexican and other Spanish language films provided an important venue for entertainment (see Arvizu, Reyes, and Pedraza, this volume). Besides hours of enjoyment, films provided Latino families with a means of helping their children stay connected with their native language and culture. Across

America where English language radio, television, and film dominated the landscape prior to the 1960s, Spanish language films exposed Latino youth to a wide variety of film genres depicting different social lifestyles, customs, and values; to an array of cultural and historical events; and to a broad range of Spanish discourses. Much like picaresque novels, Mexican movies often satirized social conventions, the lifestyles of pretentious upper classes, and illegitimate authority (Delgado & Stefancic, 2001). Spanish language films offered rich opportunities for cultural learning and cultural affirmation.

Effects of Translation on Biliteracy Development

Almost every Latino child at one time or another has taken on the role of cultural broker, translator, or interpreter for English and Spanish speakers. Although the terms *interpreter* and *translator* are used interchangeably in everyday speech, interpreting generally refers to the oral process of changing ideas from one language to another. Translation of texts, on the other hand, is a more complex process, given the reduction in the number of clues to meaning, for example, gestures, tone of voice, realia, and so on (Pam McCollum, personal communication, April 17, 2010). As a young boy, Arvizu (this volume) interpreted and translated in diverse contexts: medical offices, grocery stores, department stores, post offices, schools, churches, and other public or social agencies. Brokering communication is a challenging task requiring not only some level of fluency in the two languages but also appropriate lexicon for the various social contexts (see Arvizu, Balderrama, Fránquiz, Halcón, and Valadez, this volume). Effective translation also calls for an understanding of the speaker's intent (Vásquez, Pease-Alvarez, & Shannon, 1994). To accomplish this successfully, a language broker must stretch her limits of understanding in both languages, negotiate new vocabulary, and understand the context and the purposes of each translating event.

At least two of the contributors were tapped to play that role for an extended period of time. Although the task may be initially intimidating for young translators, there are positive benefits for the interpreter. The act of translating helps enhance vocabulary, grammar, and sociolinguistic and biliterate skills, as it did for Arvizu and Halcón (this volume).

Teachers

The majority of the narrators' teachers were White, native monolingual English speakers. Some teachers were cold and insensitive, and held deficit views of Latino students; others were genuinely good human beings, caring, sensitive, and respectful of students' cultural and ethnic backgrounds (see Balderrama, González, Mercado, Nieto, Reyes, and Valadez, this volume). Reyes (this volume) describes her elementary teachers (all nuns) as active agents in integrating Spanish in all extracurricular activities. The privileging of Spanish in school-related contexts had the powerful effect of affirming her bicultural identity and boosting her self-confidence. Songs, plays, and other school performances in Spanish fostered the development of biliteracy.

PERSISTENT THEMES ACROSS GENERATIONS: LESSONS FOR TEACHERS

Arguably, the most important lesson that can be derived from these narratives is that the traditional practice of using a mainstream lens, or a deficit-oriented, cognitive-psychological perspective (Hall, 2003, in Dudley-Marling, 2009) to evaluate the literacy and learning potential of Latinos is neither defensible nor beneficial. Judging Latino families by middle-class standards distorts and devalues the rich linguistic and cultural resources available to Latino students. It invalidates their hybrid lives, and hybrid ways of learning and engaging in literacy practices (Gutierrez, 2008). Dudley-Marling (2009) suggests that non-middle-class families should be viewed as *"differently literate* rather than *deficient* in literacy skills" (p. 1719). Continuing the practice of using a monolingual, middle-class lens to evaluate bilingual or multilingual students is an insult to their biliteracy accomplishments and to "the complexity of their thinking and representational abilities" (Maguire, 1999, p. 115).

Equally insidious is the practice of labeling Latinos "at risk" because they come from minority language homes, or speak Spanish. "At risk" implies a lack of readiness to profit from instruction. Vásquez, Pease-Alvarez, and Shannon (1994) suggest, instead, that teachers should view Latino children (and all students) as being in a "state of readiness" because a strong home language actually can strengthen learning. Nieto (this volume) endorses a similar sentiment when she urges teachers to "start where the kids are at." When a more appropriate sociocultural lens is used to evaluate Latino school children across generations, the following positive themes surface:

1. Latino parents are deeply interested in their children's education and engage them in activities that promote literacy.
2. Spanish and bilingualism is a resource, not an obstacle to literacy and learning.

3. Affirming cultural and linguistic diversity is a powerful tool for fostering academic success.
4. The effectiveness of teachers with Latino students is not dependent on teachers' fluency in Spanish.

Every generation of Latino parents, including the least educated and poorest, have taken an interest in their children's education by encouraging them to study, to maintain their Spanish, to learn English, to obey their teachers, and to take pride in their culture. Indeed, many research studies provide evidence that Latino parents engage their children in social and cultural practices that promote literacy and support children's academic development (Delgado-Gaitan, 1994; Galindo, 2001; Goldenberg, 2001; González, 2001; González, Moll, & Amanti, 2005; Guerra, 1998; Gutierrez, 2008; Moll & Dworin, 1996; Nieto, 1996; Vásquez, Pease-Alvarez, & Shannon, 1994; and others). Although parents want the best for their children and are willing to work with teachers, Dudley-Marling (2009) suggests that schools are often disrespectful or condescending regarding parents' ability to help their children. At the same time, parents may be uncertain about how schools want them to participate in literacy activities at home. School–home literacy programs, for example, often make the mistake of assuming that non-English-dominant, non-middle-class parents understand the value of such things as setting aside independent reading time. Latino parents, however, do not always understand its value and how reading time fits with homework requirements. As a result, parents may not give "just reading" high priority for their children (Dudley-Marling, 2009, p. 1737).

COMPARING MIDDLE-CLASS AND LATINO PARENTS' PRESCHOOL LITERACY PRACTICES

Similarities between middle-class preschool literacy practices and the social practices of Latino families may not be readily apparent to literacy educators, but there is remarkable likeness between the two. Middle-class families rely on the following literacy practices that provide children with a broad range of language use and experiences that support reading:

- Reading aloud to children
- Teaching nursery rhymes, songs, and finger play
- Providing access to children's books
- Taking children on trips to museums, cultural events, and historical sites

These reading readiness activities are part of the curriculum in all U.S. schools. Latino parents provide similar sociocultural practices (i.e., reading readiness) that include the following:

- Telling *cuentos* (oral stories)
- Teaching *dichos* (proverbs/sayings), *adivinanzas* (riddles), songs, and finger play in Spanish
- Providing print materials: *novelas, fotonovelas,* popular magazines, newspapers in Spanish; books, comics, newspapers, magazines in Spanish and English
- Taking their children to Spanish language films, church, and community-sponsored cultural events

The lists illustrate the kinds of activities that schools and middle-class parents value compared with the cultural literacy activities that were practiced in the narrators' homes. Except for utilizing a different language, the key elements of the literacy practices are essentially the same for both groups. Just as reading aloud to children supports oral language and vocabulary development, familiarity with book talk, and story structures, *cuentos* serve similar functions. *Cuentos*, for example, expose children to story features, *"había una vez"* ("once upon a time"), or *"Colorín, Colorado, este cuento se ha acabado"* ("Colorin, Colorado, this story is over"), story sequence, plot, characters, the problem and solution, and sometimes even a moral. Interaction between the storyteller and the listeners often takes place, clarifying and embellishing events to create dramatic effect. Whenever possible, teachers should draw on these social and cultural practices of Latino families to enhance their students' literacy skills. An important thing to remember is that, whether they are in English or Spanish, the literacy processes are the same for all these activities. Differences are superficial and related more to the economic resources available to each group than to qualitatively different practices.

An important point to note is that in spite of these families' economic difficulties, some parents purchased encyclopedia sets or world book sets for their children. Allocating limited financial resources for these big purchases demonstrated a deep commitment and the investment Latino parents made in their children's education—even when they themselves might not have been able to read the costly texts. Understanding that these preliteracy practices take place in many minority students' homes should help persuade teachers that Latino children arrive in school with rich funds of knowledge that form a strong foundation for literacy (Goldenberg, 2001; González, 2001; González, Moll, & Amanti,

2005; Moll, 1992; Moll & Dworin, 1996). Affirming cultural and linguistic diversity is a powerful tool for fostering academic success (Nieto, 1996; Reyes, this volume).

Teachers often wonder whether they can be effective with linguistically different students when they do not speak their language or are not members of their cultural group. While speaking the same language may be advantageous and even ideal, using Spanish does not necessarily guarantee a teacher can create a child-centered learning environment that is respectful and caring. As Valadez (this volume) reveals in her narrative, native Spanish-speaking teachers can be callous; they can exhibit "unsympathetic deficit views of linguistic minority students" (Bartolomé, 2008a, p. 13), even toward students from their own cultural group. Additionally, Bartolomé (2008a) points out that "caring for and loving one's subordinated students is insufficient unless the love and care are informed by authentic respect and a desire to equalize unequal learning conditions in school" (p. 2).

As the narratives reveal, teachers who did not coddle or feel sorry for their Latino students because they were poor, or because they lacked English proficiency, were the ones who were better at helping their students achieve academically. It is important to note that most of the narrators in this volume did not have a Latina/o teacher until they were in college, and even then they had only one or two professors. The key to teachers' effectiveness with Latinos was not only their "authentic caring" (Valenzuela, 1999), but their ability to challenge students to reach their potential and satiate their learning curiosity. A teacher's "authentic caring" can have a transformative effect on students' motivation to learn and on their staying power in school. Students know when teachers care about them. Even young children in the primary grades can "read" a teacher's body language and tone of voice. They can tell whether it is respectful or dismissive; no translation is needed.

The personal narratives in *Words Were All We Had: Becoming Biliterate Against the Odds* illustrate that biliteracy often emerges naturally and without much fanfare. In the case of these authors, no formal, consistent program of instruction for Spanish literacy took place at home. Parents and children simply went about their lives, interacting with those around them and developing whatever skills were needed to navigate the complex bicultural environments in which they lived. Biliteracy occurred not as a result of didactic practices, but as a spontaneous response to the situated contexts in which they found themselves. As they became more proficient in English, English seemed to support the development of their biliteracy, not the other way around (Moll & Dworin, 1996; see also Mercado, this volume). Biliteracy evolved over time as linguistic demands became more complex, as individuals matured and moved up the grades, and as individuals exerted personal agency to reach academic and professional levels in both languages.

The fact that these Chicana/o and Puerto Rican authors emerged as biliterate despite attending schools in a climate of rejection and under the threat of punishment for speaking Spanish is a testament to their resilience and tenacity. They stood firm, refusing to "trade their language and identity for basic rights" (Zentella, 1997, p. 14)—a right to a good education and a right to be who they were and what they could become. In the end, they became bicultural, bilingual, and biliterate.

References

Anzaldua, G. (1987). *Borderlands/La Frontera: The new Mestiza*. San Francisco: Spinters, Aunt Lute.

Bartolomé, L. I. (2008a). Authentic cariño and respect in minority education: The political and ideological dimensions of love. *International Journal of Critical Pedagogy, 1*(1), 1–17.

Bartolomé, L. I. (2008b). *Ideologies in education: Unmasking the trap of teacher neutrality*. New York: Peter Lang.

Bartolomé, L. I., & Balderrama, M. V. (2001). The need for educators with political and ideological clarity: Providing our children with "the best". In M. de la Luz Reyes & J. J. Halcón (Eds.), *The best for our children: Critical perspectives on literacy for Latino students* (pp. 48–64). New York: Teachers College Press.

Bradunas, E., & Toppings, B. (Eds.). (1988). *Ethnic heritage and language schools in America* [Studies in American Folklife, No. 4]. Washington, DC: U.S. Government Printing Office.

Carter, T. P. (1970). *Mexican Americans in school: A history of educational neglect.* New York: College Entrance Examination Board.

Clark, M. M. (1976). *Young fluent readers: What can they teach us?* London: Heinemann.

Cortés, L. (2000). I remember. In S. Nieto (Ed.), *Puerto Rican students in U.S. schools* (p. 3). Mahwah, NJ: Lawrence Erlbaum.

Crawford, J. (1992). *Hold your tongue: Bilingualism and the politics of "English only."* Binghamton, NY: Addison-Wesley.

Cummins, J. (1981). The role of primary language development in promoting educational success for language minority students. In California State Department of Education (Ed.), *Schooling and language minority students: A theoretical framework* (pp. 3–49). Los Angeles: Evaluation, Dissemination and Assessment Center, California State University.

Cummins, J. (1989). *Empowering minority students*. Sacramento: California Association for Bilingual Education.

Del Valle, S. (1998). Bilingual education for Puerto Ricans in New York City: From hope to compromise. *Harvard Educational Review, 68*(2), 193–217.

Delgado, R., & Stefancic, J. (2001). *Critical race theory*. New York: New York University Press.

Delgado Bernal, D. (2002). Critical race theory, LatCrit theory, and critical raced-gendered epistemologies: Recognizing students of color as holders and creators of knowledge. *Qualitative Inquiry, 8*(1), 105–126.

Delgado-Gaitan, C. (1994). Sociocultural change through literacy: Toward the empowerment of families. In B. M. Ferdman, R. Weber, & A. G. Ramirez (Eds.), *Literacy across language and cultures* (pp. 143–169). Albany: State University of New York Press.

Deloria, V., Jr. (1984). *Aggressions of civilization: Federal Indian policy since the 1880s.* Philadelphia: Temple University Press.

Dobles, R., & Segarra, J. A. (1998). Introduction. *Harvard Educational Review, 68*(2), vii–xv.

Dudley-Marling, C. (2009). Home–school literacy connections: The perceptions of African American and immigrant ESL parents in two urban communities. *Teachers College Record, 3*(7), 1713–1752.

Durkin, D. (1966). *Children who read early: Two longitudinal studies.* New York: Teachers College Press.

Dworin, J. (2003). Insights into biliteracy development: Toward a bidirectional theory of bilingual pedagogy. *Journal of Hispanic Higher Education, 2*(2), 171–186.

Featherstone, J. (1989). To make the wounded whole. *Harvard Educational Review, 59*(3), 367–378.

Ferolito, P. (2009, November 17). Dueling over dual-language classes in Yakima Valley. *Yakima Herald-Republic.* Retrieved November 19, 2009, from http//www.yakima-herald.com

Fishman, J. (1976, May). *International sociological perspectives on bilingual education.* Keynote address at the annual meeting of the National Association for Bilingual Education, San Antonio, TX.

Fishman, J. (1989). *Language and ethnicity: A minority sociolinguistic perspective.* Clevedon, England: Multilingual Matters.

Galindo, R. (2001). Family literacy in the autobiographies of Chicana/o bilingual teachers. In M. A. Gallego & S. Hollingsworth (Eds.), *What counts as literacy: Challenging the school standard* (pp. 252–270). New York: Teachers College Press.

Goldenberg, C. (2001). Making schools work for low-income families in the 21st century. In S. B. Newman & D. K. Kickinsn (Eds.), *Handbook of early literacy research* (pp. 211–231). New York: Guilford Press.

González, N. (2001). *I am my language: Discourses of women and children in the borderlands.* Tucson: University of Arizona Press.

González, N., Moll, L. C., & Amanti, C. (2005). *Funds of knowledge: Theorizing practices in households, communities, and classrooms.* Mahwah, NJ: Lawrence Earlbaum.

Gorman, M. B. (1973). *Language policy in Puerto Rican education.* Unpublished dissertation, American University, Washington, DC.

Griego Jones, T. (1993, April). *Assessing students' perceptions of biliteracy in a two-way bilingual classroom.* Paper presented at the annual meeting of the American Educational Research Association, Atlanta.

Guerra, J. C. (1998). *Close to home: Oral and literate practices in a transnational Mexicano community.* New York: Teachers College Press.

Gutierrez, K. D. (2008). Developing a sociocritical literacy in the third space. *Reading Research Quarterly, 43*(2), 148–164.

Halcón, J. J. (2001). Mainstream ideology and literacy instruction for Spanish-speaking children. In M. de la Luz Reyes & J. J. Halcón (Eds.), *The best for our children: Critical perspectives on literacy for Latino students* (pp. 65–77). New York: Teachers College Press.

Heath, S. B. (1983). *Ways with words.* New York: Cambridge University Press.

Hornberger, N. H. (1990). Creating successful learning contexts for bilingual literacy. *Teachers College Record, 92*(2), 212–229.

Hornberger, N. H. (Ed.). (2003). *Continua of biliteracy: An ecological framework for educational policy, research, and practice in multilingual settings.* Clevedon, England: Multilingual Matters.

Hornberger, N. H., & Skilton-Sylvester, E. (2003). Revisiting the continua of biliteracy: International and critical perspectives. In N. H. Hornberger (Ed.), *Continua of biliteracy: An ecological framework for educational policy, research, and practice in multilingual settings* (pp. 35–67). Clevedon, England: Multilingual Matters.

Kilgannon, C. (2004, August, 2). The neighborhood ties that still bind. *New York Times,* p. B4.

Macías, R. (1994). Inheriting sins while seeking absolution: Language diversity and national statistical data sets. In D. Spener (Ed.), *Adult biliteracy in the United States* (pp. 15–45). McHenry, IL: Center for Applied Linguistics.

Maguire, M. (1999). A bilingual child's choices and voices: Lessons in noticing, listening, and understanding. In E. Franklin (Ed.), *Reading and writing in more than one language: Lessons for teachers* (pp. 115–149). Alexandria, VA: TESOL.

Meier, D., & Wood, G. (Eds.). (2004). *Many children left behind: How the No Child Left Behind Act is damaging our children and schools.* Boston: Beacon.

Moll, L. C. (1992). Bilingual classrooms and community analysis: Some recent trends. *Educational Researcher, 21*(2), 20–24.

Moll, L. C., & Dworin, J. (1996). Biliteracy development in classrooms: Social dynamics and cultural possibilities. In D. Hicks (Ed.), *Discourse, learning, and schooling* (pp. 221–246). Cambridge, MA: Cambridge University Press.

Nieto, S. (1996). *Affirming diversity: The sociopolitical context of multicultural education* (2nd ed.). White Plains, NY: Longman.

Nieto, S. (1998). Fact and fiction: Stories of Puerto Ricans in U.S. Schools. *Harvard Educational Review, 68*(2), 133–163.

Pak, H. R. (2003). When MT is L2: The Korean Church school as a context for cultural identity. In N. H. Hornberger (Ed.), *Continua of biliteracy: An ecological framework for educational policy, research, and practice in multilingual settings* (pp. 269–290). Clevedon, England: Multilingual Matters.

Pausada, A. (2008). Puerto Rico, school language policies. In J. M. González (Ed.), *Encyclopedia of bilingual education* (Vol. 2, pp. 701–704). Thousand Oaks, CA: Sage.

Ramírez, A. G. (1994). Sociolinguistic considerations in biliteracy planning. In D. Spener (Ed.), *Adult biliteracy in the United States* (pp. 47–70). McHenry, IL: Center for Applied Linguistics.

Reyes, M. de la Luz. (2001). Unleashing possibilities: Biliteracy in the primary grades. In M. de la Luz Reyes & J. J. Halcón (Eds.), *The best for our children: Critical perspectives on literacy for Latino students* (pp. 96–121). New York: Teachers College Press.

Reyes, M. de la Luz. (2004, April). *The power of linguistic affirmation: A child's personal journey to biliteracy*. Paper presented at the annual meeting of the American Educational Research Association, San Diego.

Reyes, M. de la Luz. (2008). Languages in colonial schools, western. In J. M. González (Ed.), *Encyclopedia of bilingual education* (Vol. 1, pp. 483–489). Thousand Oaks, CA: Sage.

Reyes, M. de la Luz, & Costanzo, L. C. (2002). On the threshold of biliteracy: A first graders' personal journey. In L. D. Soto (Ed.), *Making a difference in the lives of bilingual/bicultural children* (pp. 145–156). New York: Peter Lang.

Reyes, M. de la Luz, Laliberty, E. A., & Orbanosky, J. A. (1993). Emerging biliteracy and cross-cultural sensitivity in a language arts classroom. *Language Arts, 70*(8), 38–47.

Rodriguez, R. (1982). *Hunger of memory: The education of Richard Rodriguez*. New York: Bantam Dell.

San Miguel, G., Jr. (1987). *Let them all take heed: Mexican Americans and the campaign for educational equality in Texas, 1910–1981*. Austin: University of Texas Press.

San Miguel, G., Jr. (1999). The schooling of Mexicanos in the Southwest, 1848–1891. In J. Moreno (Ed.), *The elusive quest for equality: 150 years of Chicano/Chicana education* (pp. 31–51). Cambridge, MA: Harvard University, Harvard Educational Review.

Sánchez, R. (1995). *Telling identities: The Californio testimonios*. Minneapolis: University of Minnesota Press.

Sibley, B. (2004). Around the world of Mike Todd [documentary]. In M. Todd, *Around the World in 80 Days* [DVD, special edition]. Warner Brothers Entertainment.

Solórzano, D. G., & Yosso, T. J. (2002). Critical race methodology: Counterstory-telling as an analytical framework for education research. *Qualitative Inquiry, 8*(1), 23–44.

Street, B. (1988). Literacy, pedagogy and nationalism. *Occasional papers*. New York: Teachers College, Columbia University.

Suarez, R. (2007). Prólogo. In T. Miller (Ed.), *Como aprendí Inglés* (pp. xi–xiv). Washington, DC: National Geographic.

Taylor, D., & Dorsey-Gaines, C. (1988). *Growing up literate: Learning from inner-city families*. Portsmouth, NH: Heinemann.

Trimmer, J. F. (Ed.). (1997). *Narration as knowledge*. Portsmouth, NH: Boynton/Cook.

Trueba, H. T. (Ed.). (1987). *Success or failure: Linguistic minority children at home and at school*. New York: Harper & Row.

Tse, L. (2001). Resisting and reversing language shift: Heritage-language resilience among U.S. native biliterates. *Harvard Educational Review, 71*(4), 676–706.

U.S. Commission on Civil Rights. (1972). *The excluded student* [Report III. Educational Practices affecting Mexican Americans in the Southwest]. Washington, DC: U.S. Government Printing Office.

U.S. Commission on Civil Rights. (1976). *Puerto Ricans in the continental United States: An uncertain future*. Washington, DC: U.S. Government Printing Office.

U.S. Department of Education, National Center for Education Statistics. (2006). *Public elementary and secondary students, staff, schools, and school districts: School year 2003–04* (NCES 2006–307).

Valdés, G. (1997). Dual language immersion programs: A cautionary note concerning the education of language minority students. *Harvard Educational Review, 67*(3), 391–429.

Valenzuela, A. (1999). *Subtractive schooling: U.S.-Mexican youth and the politics of caring*. Albany: State University of New York Press.

Vásquez, O. A., Pease-Alvarez, L., & Shannon, S. H. (1994). *Pushing boundaries: Language and culture in a Mexicano community*. Cambridge, MA: Cambridge University Press.

Wong-Fillmore, L. (1991). When learning a second language means losing the first. *Early Childhood Research Quarterly, 6*, 323–347.

Yosso, T. J. (2006). *Critical race counterstories among the Chicana/Chicano educational pipeline*. New York: Routledge.

Zentella, A. C. (1997). *Growing up bilingual*. Malden, MA: Blackwell.

About the Editor
and the Contributors

María de la Luz Reyes is Professor Emerita, University of Colorado–Boulder. Her research and publications focus on development of Spanish/English biliteracy in K–12, and on equity issues in higher education. Her book, *The Best for Our Children: Critical Perspectives on Literacy for Latino Students* (with John J. Halcón), received the Critics' Choice Award from the American Educational Studies Association (AESA) in 2004.

Steven F. Arvizu earned a Ph.D. in anthropology from Stanford. He did postdoctoral work at the University of Michigan and Harvard University. He served as Dean of Graduate Studies at CSU Bakersfield, founding Provost at CSU Monterey Bay, and President of Oxnard College. As an educator, he is best known as an innovator and builder in the bilingual and cross-cultural movements and in reforming, developing, and creating educational institutions.

María V. Balderrama received her Ph.D. from Stanford University. She is Professor of Education at California State University, San Bernardino, and Director of Project WIN, a federally funded program supporting mathematics achievement and biliteracy of adolescent Latinas. Her research and publication focus on adolescent education, teachers, English learners, and equity. Her work appears in numerous journals, books, encyclopedias, and textbooks. She is co-author of *Teaching Performance Expectations for Educating English Learners* (2006).

Lilia I. Bartolomé is Professor of Applied Linguistics at the University of Massachusetts, Boston. Her research interests include the preparation of effective teachers of minority and second language learners in multicultural contexts. Her books include *Ideologies in Education: Unmasking the Trap of Teacher Neutrality; The Misteaching of Academic Discourses; Immigrant Voices: In Search of Pedagogical Equity* (with Henry Trueba); and *Dancing with Bigotry: The Poisoning of Culture* (with Donaldo Macedo).

María E. Fránquiz is Professor of Curriculum and Instruction at the University of Texas–Austin. Her research interests are bilingual/multicultural education and language/literacy studies. She co-edited *Scholars in the Field: The Challenges of Migrant Education* (with Cinthia Salinas) and *Inside the Latin@ Experience: A Latin@ Studies Reader* (with Norma E. Cantú). Fránquiz is a native of Rio Piedras, Puerto Rico.

Josué M. González is Professor of Education at Arizona State University. He has worked in various aspects of bilingual education for most of his 40-year career. He was President of the NABE and Director of the Office of Bilingual Education and Minority Languages Affairs in the U.S. Department of Education. His books include *New Concepts for New Challenges: Professional Development for Teachers of Immigrant Youth* (with Linda Darling-Hammond); editor of *Conflicts, Disputes and Tensions Between Identity Groups: What Modern School Leaders Need to Know*; and the 2-volume *Encyclopedia of Bilingual Education*.

John J. Halcón is Professor of Education at California State University, San Marcos, where he teaches bilingual, multicultural education. His research interests and publications focus on education of English language learners, racism in higher education, and Chicano/Latino education. His work on a service-learning project, Tutor Connection, received the Jimmy and Rosalynn Carter Foundation Award, and the project was designated as a Certified Carter Foundation Partner.

Carmen I. Mercado is Professor of Literacy in the Hunter College School of Education. Her major research interests include understanding uses of language and literacy in bilingual, multidialectal homes and communities. She also has worked with preservice teachers to develop on-line curriculum resources using archives of bilingual writers housed at El Centro, the leading center on educational, language, and economic issues affecting the U.S. Puerto Rican community.

Sonia Nieto is Professor of Education, University of Massachusetts, Amherst. Her research focuses on multicultural education, teacher education, and the education of Latinos, immigrants, and culturally and linguistically diverse students. Her books include *Affirming Diversity: The Sociopolitical Context of Multicultural Education* (with Patty Bode); *The Light in Their Eyes: Creating Multicultural Learning Communities*; *What Keeps Teachers Going?*; and three edited volumes: *Puerto Rican Students in U.S. Schools*, *Why We Teach*, and *Dear Paulo: Letters from Those Who Dare Teach*.

Pedro Pedraza is a founding staff member of El Centro de Estudios Puertorriqueños at Hunter College, CUNY, which focuses on the experience, art, history, culture, and language of the mainland Puerto Rican community. He has served on several boards that advocate for children and youth in East Harlem. He is also the founder of El Barrio Popular Education Project, The Puerto Rican/Latino Education Roundtable, and the National Latino/a Education Research and Policy Project (based at University of Texas–Austin, with Angela Valenzuela, Director).

Concepción M. Valadez is Professor of Education at UCLA. She has a B.A. from UC Berkeley. Her M.A. and Ph.D. are from Stanford University in Linguistics and Curriculum and Instruction. Her areas of expertise are bilingualism and literacy and the relationship between mathematics and language development. In 2005, she was awarded a UCLA Rosenfield Prize for her Los Angeles inner-city work on basic literacy education for Latino immigrants.

Index